Mitji–Let's Eat!

Mi'kmaq Recipes from Sikniktuk

By Margaret Augustine & Lauren Beck

NIMBUS PUBLISHING
NIMBUS.CA

Nimbus Publishing Limited
3660 Strawberry Hill Street, Halifax, NS, B3K 5A9
(902) 455-4286 nimbus.ca

Nimbus Publishing is based in Kjipuktuk, Mi'kma'ki, the traditional territory of the Mi'kmaq People.

Printed and bound in Canada

Editor: Valerie Mansour
Editor for the press: Whitney Moran
Design: Heather Bryan
NB1700

The authors and publisher would like to express sincere thanks to Mount Allison University for a generous donation that helped make this project possible.

Research for this project was sponsored by the Social Sciences and Humanities Research Council.

Library and Archives Canada Cataloguing in Publication

Title: Mitji--let's eat! : Mi'kmaq recipes from Sikniktuk / by Margaret Augustine & Lauren Beck.
Other titles: Let's eat! | Mi'kmaq recipes from Sikniktuk
Names: Augustine, Margaret, author. | Beck, Lauren, author.
Description: Includes index.
Identifiers: Canadiana (print) 20230229859 | Canadiana (ebook) 20230229921 |
ISBN 9781774712276 (softcover) | ISBN 9781774712283 (EPUB)
Subjects: LCSH: Cooking—New Brunswick. | CSH: Mi'kmaq—Food—New Brunswick. | LCGFT: Cookbooks.
Classification: LCC TX714 .A94 2023 | DDC 641.59/29734307151—dc23

Nimbus Publishing acknowledges the financial support for its publishing activities from the Government of Canada, the Canada Council for the Arts, and from the Province of Nova Scotia. We are pleased to work in partnership with the Province of Nova Scotia to develop and promote our creative industries for the benefit of all Nova Scotians.

We dedicate this book in memory
of contributors who have passed:
Eunice Augustine, Elizabeth Levi,
John Levi, and Herman John Simon.

—MA & LB

Table of Contents

The Flag of Elsipogtog First Nation against the background of the Richibucto River in New Brunswick.

Introduction to the Foodways of Sikniktuk

*M*itji—*Let's Eat!* The welcome call heard by children, hungry workers, family, and friends when dinner is ready defines the purpose of this book as one that invites you to bring people together to celebrate and practice Mi'kmaq foodways.

By foodways, we are referring to the recipes passed down from one generation to the next, and the ways in which traditional foods and medicines are gathered, hunted, and cooked. What is eaten—when and where—provides us with insight from ancestors and Elders about how to nourish the spirit and body through Mi'kmaw culture and knowledge.

Mitji—Let's Eat! Mi'kmaq Recipes from Sikniktuk is more than a cookbook offering authentic and popular Mi'kmaq recipes using ingredients found in one of Canada's most vibrant Indigenous communities. Our objective is to pass on to you, the readers, the wisdom the Elders have shared with us.

Siknitkuk is one of the seven traditional districts which includes Elsipogtog First Nation, a community of over three thousand; Lnoo Minigoo (Indian Island First Nation); Tjipogtotig (Bouctouche First Nation); and Amlamgog (Fort Folly First Nation). L'nu Mniku (Lennox Island First Nation) in Prince Edward Island forms part of the traditional districut of Epekwitk aq Piktuk.

This book is for everyone—a young mother who has never cooked a Mi'kmaw dish, a single

Irving Peterpaul teaches the authors how to fish on the frozen Richibucto River.

Elder Anita Joseph.

person living alone who hasn't had a family meal in a while, or a nascent foodie keen to get started. The recipes explain both traditional and contemporary means of preparing seasonal dishes using local ingredients, whether that is in Sackville, New Brunswick, or Elsipogtog First Nation. To make a return to traditional ingredients even more appealing, we have done research among the Elders about how flavour is best developed. They share advice about how to deal with the gaminess of wild meat, how to make use of parts of animals, fish, and lobster that often get discarded, and how to modify or extend recipes to feed more people in a pinch.

Mitji! offers an important source for scholars or historians interested in learning more about the Mi'kmaq as a people with deep culinary wisdom and experience. This history looks to community-based knowledge rather than history books. The recipes paint a picture of how Mi'kmaq foodways were influenced by colonization on the one hand, and how food became and remains a significant vehicle of resistance on the other. For instance, we explore the Atlantic coast fisheries, examine some of the historical issues that have given rise to conflicts between Mi'kmaq and settler people, and try to build bridges by sharing knowledge that contextualizes Mi'kmaw fishing and hunting practices, as well as the Mi'kmaq's inherent rights. We discuss government involvement in altering those foodways, and reveal how First Nations communities have found creative ways of restoring them.

The land of the Mi'kmaq, Mi'kma'ki, covers part of New Brunswick and all of Nova Scotia, Prince Edward Island, and Newfoundland, also part of Quebec and Maine, and while this book focuses on Sikniktuk, these recipes will seem familiar to Mi'kmaq elsewhere. The book's geographical scope underlines the interconnected foodways of the region, with Mi'kmaq regularly going to Maine to pick potatoes, in what also reveals the seasonal activities that contribute to Mi'kmaq culture and foodways—even today.

The Mi'kmaw name Sikniktuk means "drainage land," and anybody who has spent time in this region of Canada will immediately understand why—the area is characterized by the salt marshes and brackish rivers that meet the Northumberland Strait separating New Brunswick from Prince Edward Island, and from the shores of the Bay of Fundy. The Acadians diked many of these marshes to make way for arable land, but the relationship between the Mi'kmaq in the region and their traditional territory has remained strong, despite challenges posed by colonization.

Charlotte Rhoda Levi enjoying a slice of Apple Pie (see p. 50).

(see p. 50)

Most Mi'kmaq communities are on, or near, water where residents can fish, or they are beside, or within, forested areas where they can hunt. Not far away are settlers whose relationship with the land can be quite different, in that they may never have tried fishing or hunting for their own food. This book explores the intercultural encounters that have come to inform Mi'kmaw and other regional cuisines with their global reaches to Asia, Europe, and Latin America. At the same time, we will see the influence that Indigenous ingredients have had on an international stage.

We have created an intergenerational source of wisdom that combines a cultural history of Mi'kmaw cuisine with a practical cookbook, while emphasizing the authority and cultural memory that the Elders and Knowledge Holders in Sikniktuk bring to their communities. We will focus on the ingredients, their history, and how they are used today. We have collected stories about particular foods that reveal both humorous and difficult culinary experiences. For instance, eel, molasses, and lobster

Pan-fried smelts fished from the Richibucto River.

have complex and sacred histories. Each recipe is contextualized with background on its origins, pertinent sidebars, biographical information about the contributors or key actors in their lives, food stories shared by our contributors, and, of course, detailed instructions for the preparation of each dish.

The authors interviewed community members whose cultural practices, including the ability to share their learnings and experiences, were threatened by residential school and other colonial policies. We have given Elders and Knowledge Holders from several Mi'kmaq communities, with connections to Sikniktuk, the opportunity to tell their life stories, their memories about food growing up, their personal reflections on how food has changed over the years, and the impacts of colonization on Mi'kmaw cuisine. They also share a significant recipe in their lives—one that they are known for doing well or that was passed down through the generations and is venerated within the community. Some of their stories are personal, intense, humorous, and educational—and all were given with a generosity of spirit so that others can learn from them.

At Elsipogtog, and in any other Mi'kmaw community, everybody knows who makes the best L'nu taco or meat pie. This book, for the first time, brings together these signature dishes. *Mitji!* returns these teachings to the community so that the next generation of home cooks will benefit, as will others interested in Atlantic and Indigenous foodways. The region's settler population also uses the same ingredients, but often in different ways. By telling these stories, we also hope to weave together intercultural understandings of often disparate communities.

The book builds upon models for disseminating Indigenous food knowledge trailblazed by writers such as John Wisdomkeeper in *Native Recipes from the Grandmothers* (2013) and Barrie Kavasch in *Native Harvests: American Indian Wild Foods and Recipes* (2013). Other works, including *La patate cadeau, ou La "vraie" histoire de la poutine râpée: un conte* (2014), are directed at younger demographics. These are excellent sources for further reading.

We organized the book to reflect the seasonal relationship between the Mi'kmaq and their foodways, so the first four sections feature dishes that are popular in the spring, summer, fall, and winter months, while the fifth section offers year-round dishes. Some sections have more recipes than others, as fresh, local ingredients are less plentiful in the early spring as compared to the fall and winter. Opening each section is a story woven from the Elders' words that sheds insight on the season or an ingredient. Each recipe is paired with a quote from its contributor offering advice or sharing a food experience. We also have included brief explanations about a range of subjects—from how fats have been used, to what sorts of ingredients the Indian Agent gave to Mi'kmaq families. The final section offers a summary of Indigenous ingredients and cooking methods.

The Authors

Co-authors of Mitji, *Margaret Augustine and Dr. Lauren Beck, in Elsipogtog.*

Margaret Augustine was born in Malta and first made a connection with Atlantic Canada when she started her Master's degree in Island Studies at the University of Prince Edward Island, which is where she met her now-husband, Dr. Patrick Augustine, of Elsipogtog First Nation. Margaret has been a community member in Elsipogtog for many years. There, she has taught in the Aotiitj programme, which is designed for youth interested in pursuing higher education at St. Thomas University, and she has spent much time among the Elders in the community learning from their wisdom. She is currently teaching at the University of Prince Edward Island.

Dr. Lauren Beck came to the Atlantic region when she was hired as a professor by Mount Allison University in Sackville, New Brunswick. She researches visual and material culture of the Atlantic world and teaches courses on food and on subjects relating to settler colonialism and decolonization. She is married to Rob LeBlanc (St. Thomas University), who teaches in the Aotiitj programme at Elsipogtog First Nation. She has published several books on Indigenous culture and colonialism.

Acknowledgements

This book would not have been possible without the support of colleagues, friends, and mentors, in addition to financial support from Oetjgoapeniag Elnoei Family Services of Elsipogtog First Nation, Mount Allison University, the University of Prince Edward Island, the Social Sciences and Humanities Research Council, and the Canada Research Chairs program.

We wish to acknowledge the contributions of key people. Elder Anita Joseph (Elsipogtog First Nation) served as our liaison with many of the Elders interviewed for this book. She attended the interviews, exchanged thoughts, helped to jog their memories, and translated concepts from Mi'kmaw into English for us (and vice versa). She also helped us vet this book's contents with the contributors. Her edits and theirs have proven to be vital to the editing process.

Elder Gary Joe Augustine and his granddaughter Trinity Augustine in the longhouse at Elsipogtog.

Dr. Patrick Augustine.

Mrs. Rhoda Francis (standing) and her sister Mrs. Laura Barlow (sitting). Quite a number of recipes in the cookbook originate from these two beautiful ladies.

We wish to also thank Dr. Patrick Augustine (Elsipogtog First Nation and Assistant Professor of Indigenous Studies, University of Prince Edward Island), who has been a consultant on this project because of his vast knowledge of the community and his people's history.

Two students performed the difficult task of transcribing all recorded interviews—Gabrielle Barlow (Indian Island First Nation and Dalhousie University) and Desirée Boulanger (Mount Allison University). Without these transcriptions, we could never have seen the complex connections that emerged from the Elders' interviews.

Gary Simon (Elsipogtog First Nation) is an Elder, Mi'kmaq language specialist, and Knowledge Sharer

Photographer Patricia Bourque on the Richibucto River, winter 2023.

in Sikniktuk who provided linguistic support on Mi'kmaq orthography.

Several individuals contributed in important ways to the production of this book—among them Debra Williams, who lent us dishes for staging the recipes, and Jasmine Pauze, who helped us organize the winter photoshoot. We also must acknowledge the beautiful and inspiring work of Patricia Bourque, our photographer.

We acknowledge the generous investment that Nimbus Publishing, our publisher, is making in our book. They are committed to ensuring that Mi'kmaw knowledge is available to the next generation and have created an excellent forum for publishing unique food histories and cookbooks. We wish to also thank Whitney Moran for her time shaping this project with us, and Valerie Mansour for her editorial and subject-matter expertise.

And finally, we must acknowledge the passing of contributors who greatly influenced this book. Uncle Herman passed away in 2022 after a long and storied life, which he generously shared with us shortly before his passing, and in 2023 the community lost War Chief John Levi. We are honoured to have worked with these and the remaining contributors and hope that this book brings their voices to life in perpetuity.

Spring

The Story of Falling into the Well

Lucy was raised by her grandparents along with a bunch of siblings and cousins on Hill Street in Big Cove (the place name was changed in the early 2000s to Elsipogtog First Nation). All of them, even the young ones, had their own job to do each day in Mi'giju's (grandmother's) enormous garden—harvest and clean carrots for dinner, pick and shell late-summer peas, weed around the beets, and in spring prepare for summer.

One spring, when Lucy was six, her job was to fetch water for Mi'giju's prized tomato plant. She'd grown them for decades from the previous year's seeds; each year they were started in the kitchen in March to plant in the garden once it was warm enough in June. Most houses in Elsipogtog at that time used well water retrieved by hand from a nearby well.

As she had for the previous two months, one day Lucy went off to the well with her bucket to collect water, and return home to feed Mi'giju's tomato plant. Her grandparents were out fishing and her favourite nsukwi (aunt), Agnes, accompanied her and her brother Andrew to the well, which was located inside the small shed that protected it. They decided to have a picnic by the well, which overlooked the Richibucto River and afforded them a magnificent view of the water, which that day was so still that it reflected the fluffy clouds and the infinite blue sky.

After her nsukwi ran back to the house to make sandwiches for them to eat, Lucy remembered her job and approached the well, bucket in hand. Andrew, who was playing by himself inside the well's shed, burst out to surprise his sister. The door swung outward from two hinges placed in parallel above the door, with Andrew soaring out over Lucy's head to land square on the picnic blanket in a fit of giggles. Lucy turned around excitedly only to be met with the door as it swung closed, hitting her square in the face and pushing her backward.

Lucy called out to her brother, who rushed into the shed to find his sister at the bottom of an ice-coated well with no way to get out. The butter was swinging perilously from a rope, and the neighbour's cream was long gone, surely knocked along with Lucy down into the well's dark vanishing point.

Agnes arrived at that moment and quickly appraised what needed to happen next. She ran to her father's barn nearby and found a ladder, which she heaved onto the shed and, using an axe, cut an opening in the roof of the shed large enough for her to hoist a second ladder inside, which she directed straight into the well. Lucy, stunned by the cold, or possibly by the butter landing on her head, still managed to find her way up the ladder and into her aunt's warm arms.

She doesn't remember much of what happened after falling into the well until she woke up in the house, insulated with the warmth of blankets and family. The doctor had already left—she had sustained a concussion, either from the flying door or from one of the other hard substances she met on the way down. After that experience, Lucy's job was upgraded to a somewhat safer role as flour specialist when Mi'giju' prepared their daily bread.

Eel Stew

Elizabeth Levi

The humble eel is one of the most plentiful fish found in New Brunswick's lakes and rivers, and a traditional food for both the Mi'kmaq and settlers. Georgina Barlow of Indian Island First Nation remembers how popular they were when she was younger: "People from Big Cove would come down here and spear eels; you could see their boat lights go by at night from the shore." It's been a while since she's seen anybody's lamps at night during eel season, although eels can be fished after the sun sets until it rises in the morning year-round. They are particularly tasty in the spring, just before the ice thaws. Some people find that eel tastes like lobster, whereas others swear the flavour is like chicken!

Don't be afraid to try partridge— it tastes like chicken! –Elizabeth Levi

The American eel is the most common variety found in the region and they grow up to two to three feet in length, a perfect size to enjoy for a family meal. Their lithe bodies make them strong swimmers, which gives their flesh a slightly firmer texture when cooked.

To clean them, remove both the innards and then the skin. For this last step, make a partial incision across the top of the fish's head, then double the loosened head backward along the length of the body for three or four inches. You can use newspaper to get a better grip on the fish while removing the skin.

If desired, reserve the head and tail to prepare a broth for this recipe. Place in a pot, cover with water, simmer twenty to thirty minutes, then strain before using.

This dish features layered eel and vegetables, crowned with a golden crust.

> **Eel Ground** in Northern New Brunswick is named after the fish found in abundance there. Its traditional name, Natoaganeg, comes from natuamk, meaning spearing eels through the ice. The reserve was established in 1783, although Mi'kmaq have lived in the region since time immemorial. Eel Ground and Indian Island are only separated by fifty-five miles, but their culinary traditions vary widely. For example, boiled dinner in Eel Ground includes ribs, whereas moose neckbones are used in Indian Island.

The Richibucto River at sunset.

Serves 4
Preparation time:
1 hour, 15 minutes

----

1 eel, cleaned, cut
    in half, then
    lengthwise in 4
    portions
1/2 cup (125 ml) water
    or eel stock
1 tsp (5 ml) salt
1/2 recipe of Lu'sknikn
    dough (see p. 99)
4 medium potatoes,
    finely sliced
1 onion, finely sliced
1/2 tsp (2 ml) black
    pepper

Eel Stew RECIPE

Preheat the oven to 350°F (175°C).

Place eel portions in a casserole dish, cover with water or stock, and season with 1/2 tsp (2 ml) salt. Bake for 30 minutes until browned.

Prepare Lu'sknikn dough and roll it out in the shape of the casserole dish.

Remove eel from the oven and layer potatoes and onion slices on top and season with pepper and remaining salt.

Cover the casserole dish with Lu'sknikn dough and bake uncovered for 30 minutes. Your eel stew is ready to be enjoyed when the dough turns golden brown.

Elder Elizabeth Levi was born in the woods, in the hills of Sussex, New Brunswick, where her mother and grandmother were spending the winter working in lumberjack camps and making baskets to sell in Moncton. Usually, they would only be there in summer. Mi'kmaq camps can still be found throughout this region of Sikniktuk, where they are used for hunting and basket making.

When Elizabeth was baptized in a chilly church decorated for Christmas, they put her on top of the church's little heater during Communion. Churches then didn't always have a lot of resources beyond spirit, faith, and community.

Jigaw (Striped Bass)

Mary Louise Joseph

People from Atlantic Canada will have heard of, if not grown up with, some form of boiled dinner. In the Maritimes, especially among Acadians, boiled dinners usually involve pork or chicken, placed in a pot with vegetables from the garden, covered with water, and simmered until everything is tender. In Elsipogtog, fish is also boiled, a traditional Mi'kmaq cooking process.

My family's fried bass recipe—well, I'd say it's better than buying it at Dixie Lee!
—Mary Louise Joseph

Striped bass (jigaw) has a texture similar to that of haddock and grows to about two feet long. It is usually fished in fast-moving water in the late spring and late fall, using the fish's preferred food sources as bait—gaspereau (herring), eel, and sometimes perch. In the Miramichi River, striped bass is considered a bycatch because it invades areas where salmon—a more valuable fish in today's markets—spawns.

Mary Louise remembers her father, Henry, **pan-frying bass fillets** when she was growing up. To fry them, make sure all the small bones and skin have been removed, dry each fillet with a paper towel, dredge in a mixture of flour, salt, and pepper, then gently shake to remove any excess flour. Pour oil into a frying pan and place on high heat. Once the oil shimmers, fry each fillet until golden brown on both sides. Serve with a sprinkle of salt, if desired, and a squeeze of lemon.

Bass heads and tails are reserved to make stock.

Undated photo of Mali Malgalit (Mary Margaret) Dedam (Sock) & Henry Dedam, Mary Louise Joseph's parents.

Harvesters in this region of New Brunswick organize annual bass derbies as they now consider fishing striped bass an important means of protecting salmon. Fisher and War Chief of Elsipogtog John Levi remembers the first derby a few years ago when six hundred bass were caught. Not wanting to waste any, he found himself in a pickle. How could he make use of so many fish? He found someone to clean and preserve them for freezing in family-sized portions and located a spare freezer in the community to store them. "I gave those out all winter long from our freezer," says John. "People could just go in and take what they wanted or needed."

That bass would have come from the Richibucto River, west of Elsipogtog First Nation. In fact, where the river splits near Targettville, the northern-most branch is called Bass River—and for good reason. Many community members recall fishing for bass on a cold night while growing up in Elsipogtog. One remembers feeling a tug on the net and, without a lot of light, excitedly pulling it toward them into the boat to appraise the size of their catch only to come face-to-face with an eel, which they called "freshwater snakes." Eel attract bass, so it is not uncommon for them to be caught at the same time—the fisher must be prepared for any surprises.

Indian Island, called Lno Minigoo, is located off the coast of New Brunswick just south of Rexton at the mouth of the Richibucto River. Indian Island First Nation is on the mainland across the water from the original Indian Island. Indian Island First Nation claim it as theirs and, while no settlers live there, traditionally the island has been a rich source of cranberries and a place where families would camp to fish. Anne Barlow remembers that the island has burial grounds, a dancing circle, and it once had a chapel and several dwellings. There are many Mi'kmaq objects on the island, a testament to their long-standing presence there.

Jigaw (Striped Bass) RECIPE

This dish features two Native ingredients—bass and potatoes—that have been part of the Mi'kmaw diet since before European contact. Mary Louise Joseph, who shared this recipe, recalled that her father loved cooking fish—he'd sometimes fry bass. But his favourite way to prepare it was boiled with potatoes, and he would always invite along the person who gave him the fish so that they could enjoy it too.

After removing the skin, head, and tail—reserving the head and tail for the stock—the bass is cut along the width of its body, leaving the bones intact. When boiled, the bones contribute a richness to the dish and ensure that all parts of the fish go into the meal. Place the head, tail, and any remaining meat in a pot and cover with water; cover the pot with a lid and bring to a boil, then reduce to a simmer for 20–30 minutes. Strain.

This dish can also be prepared with mackerel, salmon, or cod. If using salt cod, which is how Geraldine Sock prepares this recipe (she also incorporates fried salt pork and its fat), be sure to desalinate the fish first!

Serves 4
Preparation time:
40 minutes

- -

1 striped bass, cleaned
4 large potatoes, peeled and cut into 1-inch (2.5-cm) cubes
6 cups (1.5 L) water or bass stock
1 tsp (5 ml) salt
1 large onion, sliced

Slice each bass fillet into 1-inch- (2.5-cm-) thick pieces.

Place fish and potatoes in two separate medium pots. Cover both with water, divide salt between them, and put on high heat.

Once at a rolling boil, reduce both pots to medium-low, cover with lids, and cook for 20 minutes.

When potatoes are tender, strain both and serve in separate dishes topped with raw onion and additional seasoning, if desired.

Serve with Chow Chow (see p. 62) or pickled beets.

For a satisfying variation, add a handful of cubed salt pork that has been fried in a separate pan in 2 tbsp (30 ml) oil. Drizzle the flavoured oil over the plate of striped bass and potatoes.

After making stock and cleaning up the dishes, all **fish-related leftovers** that you might consider throwing in the trash can be mashed in a bowl and then sprinkled in the vegetable garden. Fish is a quality fertilizer and can be tilled into the soil before planting tomatoes, onions, beets, and carrots in the spring, and crops such as garlic in the fall.

Fish Cakes

Geraldine Sock

Just as tuna is known as "chicken of the sea" in some parts of North America, cod is also known as "chicken haddie" in the North Atlantic region. The word haddie originates from Scotland where it refers to haddock, which is usually smoked and sometimes salted, making it ideal for fish cakes and preserving. With Scottish immigration to Atlantic Canada, haddie entered the lexicon and has taken on a life of its own.

Cans of chicken haddie contain a mixture of white fish that has been deboned and cooked, including hake, pollock, cod, and sometimes haddock. Despite not always containing haddock, it is still known as haddie and is a key ingredient for many fish cakes and chowders. Geraldine Sock prefers hers made from smoked cod, and because it's smoked, the flavour and texture is somewhat different from salt cod, although both make top-notch fish cakes.

My mother was such a good cook. One time she whipped up cod and potatoes, my favourite, and she served a bunch for Dad, some for me, and I finished mine, so when Dad had left the table for something, I took the rest of his!
–Geraldine Sock

Even though her husband was a fisher, Geraldine's mother used chicken haddie for the following recipe because it could be conveniently procured from local shops and, unlike salt cod, it does not need to desalinate overnight. (And being from Elsipogtog, Geraldine's father fished bass, mackerel, salmon, and other common species.)

Cod is less available today because of the collapse of the North Atlantic cod fishing industry in the 1990s due to overfishing. It was restricted on the global market, with other fish replacing it in the composition of chicken haddie.

In Mi'kmaw, **peju** is the term for both cod and chicken haddie. Unlike chicken, cod is a native species in the region and one that has exercised significant influence on the diet of Atlantic Canadians. The Mi'kmaq also fish crab and lobster, which work well as substitutes for chicken haddie when making fish cakes.

Fish Cakes RECIPE

Mix fish, potatoes, onion, egg, and pepper in a bowl and shape into 8 balls. Form into patties using the palms of your hands, but be careful not to overmix so the fish cakes don't fall apart.

Mix flour and salt together. Place patties on a plate, coat them with flour mixture, gently shaking off any excess flour.

Fish Cakes with Homemade Beans and Chow Chow.

Melt butter in a large saucepan on medium heat. When it starts to bubble, place patties and fry for 4 minutes on each side, then remove to paper towel before serving.

Fish Cakes can be served with Pipnaqn (p. 110), Homemade Beans (p. 113), Chow Chow (p. 62), and a cup of black tea, or dipped in apple-sauce or molasses.

> **Fish cakes** can be made with pretty much any cooked fish, or with fish that has been smoked or salted. The firmer texture from these processes keeps the fish from being too mushy while working the potato-fish mixture into patties. Cooked, smoked, and salted fish also will have less moisture than the raw ingredient. Leftover fish of any sort (trout, salmon, bass, and even scallop, crab, and lobster) can be put aside, frozen, or used the next day for fish cakes.

> Gordon Francis, Geraldine's brother, remembers how **cod** used to come in bundles of fifteen or so whole salted fish. Their family would eat cod at least once a week as it was an inexpensive source of protein that could be procured easily in any grocery store. It is now more expensive and comes in much smaller quantities. Salt cod can also be difficult to source outside of Atlantic Canada, with some supermarkets often stocking products that contain cod bits rather than fillets or the entire fish.

Serves 4
Preparation time: 35 minutes

397-g (14-oz) can chicken haddie (or cooked salt cod leftovers)
5 large potatoes, boiled and mashed
1 onion, thinly sliced
1 egg
1/4 tsp (1 ml) pepper
1/2 cup (125 ml) flour
pinch of salt, if desired
3 tbsp (45 ml) butter

Markers for a Mi'kmaw vegetable garden.

Growing Food

Most people in Sikniktuk remember growing up with a garden filled with carrots, cabbage, peas, beans, onions, lettuce, potatoes, cucumbers, and tomatoes. Today their vegetables are planted in rows, just as settlers have done for centuries. This is not a traditional practice among Mi'kmaq food cultivators, even though they have planted some crops, such as corn, in rows in recent centuries.

Traditionally, Mi'kmaq have foraged for fruits (i.e., blueberries, elder–berries, blackberries, raspberries, wild strawberries, apples, chokecherries); nuts (i.e., groundnuts, acorns, beechnuts, chestnuts); and some vegetables. Otherwise, their diet was meat intensive, focused on game and fish. These foraging practices had an important influence on settler diets.

Wabanaki Peoples have always harvested fiddleheads every May. This spiral-shaped green fern is high in protein, iron, potassium, and folate. Settlers didn't notice them growing in the forest, so when the Indigenous

Peoples in the region started to sell them in the market, settlers quickly grew enamoured of the beautiful vegetable. Today it is considered a delicacy that Canadians can enjoy freshly harvested in spring, or frozen year-round. Another example can be found in maple syrup, explored elsewhere in this book.

Foraging for seasonal ingredients required the Mi'kmaq to observe how plants rely upon each other, practices that have ultimately influenced how some Mi'kmaq approach the cultivation of settler crops. For instance, Jake Sock recalls how his family did not use a trellis to grow peas, which were introduced to the region following the arrival of Europeans in the late fifteenth century. Instead, the peas grew along the ground, forming a canopy that helped to protect and nurture other crops. Jake also knew his son would want to snack on carrots. To avoid having him stomp over other vegetables to access his favourite, Jake planted carrots on an outside row. Mi'kmaw adaptability to local conditions strongly influences what sorts of ingredients they incorporate into their diets.

Gardens are fertilized today with available commercial fertilizers, but also with traditional fertilizers—compost, seaweed, and fish remains. Freda May Augustine

Raspberries and blueberries from the summer harvest.

recalls how in the spring her father would mix the family's fish leftovers and fish bones into the soil. He covered it with a thin layer of cloth or sand that keeps the birds away and encourages the fish to break down and nourish the soil. In the fall, though, he mixed seaweed into the soil before planting the next year's crops, so its nutrients would feed the soil as it rots during and after the spring thaw. And when families had horses or cows, they would use manure to fertilize the garden.

Seaweed is also a great way of maintaining the garden's moisture. After a good rainfall, cover the garden with a layer of seaweed, but if it doesn't rain for a while, water the seaweed by hand. The water seeps through and stays in the soil longer, protected by the seaweed.

Eel casserole with potatoes.

Indigenous agricultural practices can remain invisible to settlers unaware of the interconnected and traditional ecological knowledge that undergirds Mi'kmaq foodways, which take advantage of ingredients at their freshest, while preserving harvested food for the colder months. Anita Joseph remembers picking fiddleheads in May, wild strawberries in June and July, raspberries and blueberries in July and August, and hazelnuts and cranberries in September and October. While picking food to help maintain the plant for future growing seasons, it is important to leave some fruit behind for animals, whose presence promotes renewal and natural fertilization.

In Sikniktuk all life is connected. What doesn't get consumed is preserved for later, primarily through freezing, canning and pickling, and the traditional processes of drying and salting.

Harvest season also provided an opportunity for Mi'kmaq families to earn the cash required to make other purchases. Gail Barlow recalls how, during the blueberry and potato picking seasons, the entire community at Metepenagiag First Nation (Red Bank) emptied out because almost every family moved to Maine to pick potatoes. She remembers seeing families of ten to twelve children returning from Maine at the end of the potato harvest with enough cash to buy a car or truck outright—the larger the family, the greater their harvesting capacity. Due to medical conditions, Gail's family could never go away, so she had a good vantage point to see the harvest season's impact on the community, both by the absence of children and adults and the new acquisitions that appeared after they returned each October.

When food could not be grown or hunted, or provided by the Indian Agent in rations, the Mi'kmaq had two options—purchase it with cash or barter for it using another commodity. Marlene Thomas and her mother, Matilda, picked mayflowers each year in Lennox Island and then sold them to settlers who paid them handsomely. Not everybody, though, could afford to give them cash, as many settlers also struggled to make a good living, which prompted Matilda to accept whatever she needed—lard, butter, sugar, or even second-hand clothing.

These days **seaweed** can be found in expensive bales of peat to fertilize the garden. As Freda May Augustine recalls, her father would gather seaweed along the nearby shore in the fall, mix it into the soil, then plant his potatoes. In the spring, he repeated this step before planting what would become late summer and fall harvests. Seaweed was also used to cover food while cooking in the sand, and to line cavities dug into the ground or wells where food was stored to keep cool during the warmer months before fridges. Marlene Thomas also remembers seaweed as an essential item for insulating house foundations during the winter months in Lennox Island.

Summer

Mrs. Laura Barlow and Chief Peter Barlow from Indian Island First Nation, New Brunswick.

The Story of There's No Such Thing as a Free Pig

Ever since the arrival of the first Europeans, there have been concerns about how Indigenous Peoples could possibly survive without farms teaming with rows of crops, or pastures filled with cows, chickens, and the like, despite how strong and healthy they were. The federal government, even in the twentieth century, continued its attempts to remedy this perceived problem by giving animals away to entice families to become farmers and assimilate into Canadian culture. This is where our story starts.

Gail Barlow grew up in Metepenagiag First Nation (Red Bank), perched upon a hill along the Miramichi River where it forks at Sunny Corner. Her grandparents had a house here but they didn't have cows or chickens and, one day, thanks to the Government of Canada, they—like everyone else in town—got a pig. A small community of a few hundred people suddenly found itself with a significant population boom. Where would they put all these pigs without barns, fences, and fields?

Inevitably, somebody would lose their pig and everybody would help them look for it. Gail's grandfather came up with the idea of building a pen, to which they added more pigs, which only exacerbated the problem because pigs are incredibly intelligent and easily found a way to escape their enclosure, meaning there were multiple pigs on the loose in the community.

Pigs love water and are excellent swimmers. One warm summer day, several pigs triumphantly managed to escape their enclosures and formed a pack in the middle of town. The small herd then wiggled down to the shore and into the river, with half the community trying to safely manoeuvre their way down the steep hill after them. These pigs had lived on the reserve for several months, so they had substantially grown, with some weighing over one hundred pounds.

Gail's grandmother was a widow by then and could not wait for her son-in-law to return home to help them get the pigs out of the water. There was only one thing to do—into the water she went, along with Gail's aunt and several other community members. They wrangled and wrestled the slippery pigs to shore, and proudly carried them back up the hill to safety. For the pigs, safety didn't last long, as each one would have been sent to the butcher after the summer.

First Nations Peoples can see the funny elements in difficult situations. It is a survival mechanism to turn challenging moments into entertaining stories to be shared over the years. This story of the slippery pigs serves as a lesson about the problems caused by introducing non-traditional ways of life into a culture that already has perfectly fine ways of sustaining itself.

Chowder
(Lobster, Clam, or Corn)
Freda May Augustine

Most Atlantic Canadians enjoy some form of chowder—which usually contains seafood (clams, lobster, mussels, shrimp, and white fish), potatoes, cream or milk, and carrots and onions. The seasonality of these ingredients means that they are not always consumed when they are fresh, forcing us to resort to frozen or canned seafood.

Freda May Augustine's recipe for chowder celebrates ingredients when they are at their freshest. In Elsipogtog, fishers harvest modest quantities of lobster when they are in season. The harvest is normally shared with the community, while some of it is also sold to commercial distributors. Freda May remembers how people only ate the bodies when she was growing up because the tail and claws—two of the most valuable components on the global market—had already been sold to commercial distributors. To this day, lobster bodies are her preferred part of this crustacean.

When it comes to lobster, the best part is the body: take the legs off first, suck the meat out, then cut across the body diagonally—there's lots of meat in there that most people don't know about!
–Freda May Augustine

Today lobster are sometimes boiled in sea water while the fishers are at sea so they're ready to eat when they return to the community. The salty sea water brings out the flavour, so when cooking live lobster at home, just add a generous amount of salt to the water—for instance, a half cup of salt for twelve quarts (forty-eight cups) of tap water.

Social media posts and word-of-mouth exchanges spread the news about where freshly cooked lobster can be obtained in the community for free. Bring a cooler with ice and take as many whole lobster as you can eat! Eunice Augustine recalls that sometimes people would come by their house and offer them lobster, clams, striped bass, and other seafood in season. This form of sharing resources also happens during hunting season when a moose is hunted and butchered. Food traditionally is shared throughout the community and without the expectation of financial remuneration for the hunter.

Atlantic lobster boiled in salt water.

When lobster are not in season, Freda May reaches for corn, which is harvested in the Atlantic region in August and September. Fresh corn contributes a sweetness and juiciness that is often more vibrant than frozen or canned varieties—and certainly more flavourful than off-season fresh corn imported from abroad. Freda May grew up eating fresh corn harvested by her mother, and lobster caught by her grandfather and uncles. That freshness takes centre stage in this simple but delicious dish. You can make this as a lobster or corn chowder depending on your preference.

Serves 4
Preparation time:
50 minutes

- - - - - - - - - - - - - - - - - - - -

4 slices of bacon, diced
1 onion, diced
3 large potatoes, diced
1 cup (250 ml) water
1 cup (250 ml) 35% cream
1 tomato, diced if fresh, or crushed if canned (optional)
salt, to taste
14 oz (397 g) canned or fresh corn, or shelled lobster and clams

Chowder (Lobster, Clam, or Corn) RECIPE

Place bacon and onions in a pot and turn the heat to medium. Cook until bacon is brown.

Add potatoes and just enough water to cover, put the lid on, and cook until potatoes are ready—about 20 minutes.

Blend in cream gradually (and tomato, if using), as well as salt to taste, then corn (along with any liquid, if canned) or seafood (along with any liquid). Cook for 5 more minutes and serve.

White fish refers to several varieties of fish that have white flesh after they are cooked, including cod, haddock, hake, pollock, and sometimes halibut. These species tend to be leaner than oily species such as salmon, and they flake easily when cooked. You can substitute chicken haddie for a white fish of your choosing, just make sure to debone the fish first!

Blueberry Cake ("Poor Man's Cake")
Anne Barlow

When Anne Barlow and her ten siblings learned to cook growing up in Indian Island, their widowed mother would place ingredients on both sides of the table so that the children could repeat each of her steps. She also taught them other important survival skills that later served Anne well. Her mother ran the household, raised the children, and obtained everything they needed. She also kept the doors locked and asked her children to be mindful of strangers. Anne didn't learn until later that hiding under the bed and running off into the forest was not just a bit of childhood fun—her mother was protecting them from being taken to residential school. While in the woods, Anne and her siblings would pick blueberries for her mother's cooking.

Anne Barlow wearing traditional Mi'kmaw clothing made by Andrea Bear Nicholas and Gertrude Nicholas, Indian Island, August 18, 1997.

Blueberries have long been plentiful in the region, providing a significant source of nutrition for the Mi'kmaq. Wild blueberries offer more nutrients than cultivated ones and are an effective anti-inflammatory that can also help prevent cancer and cognitive decline. Harvested in July and August, blueberries can be used in both sweet and savoury dishes—whether as a jam or as barbeque sauce for moose ribs—and, of course, they can be tasty on their own.

For generations, the Mi'kmaq have migrated to take advantage of fruits and vegetables at their freshest. Entire families from the Maritimes went to Sedgwick, Maine, and its environs, to rake blueberries and to harvest potatoes. For a few weeks each year, people who did not normally interact or see each other came together in an intergenerational, seasonal community—something of a pop-up reserve.

Former chief of Elsipogtog Vincent Simon amassed more than fifty years of experience in the industry. He believes harvesting blueberries is about more than money. Earnings went toward clothes for the new school year, representing renewal. And it was most importantly about tradition and the relationships between people that were renewed each summer.

> To clean clams, my mother would put a knife in the pot and then throw the clams on top and cover with water. The next morning, all the sand had been released from the clams and would be settled around the knife at the bottom of the pot.
> –Anne Barlow

The Mi'kmaq, however, have gone less often to Maine in recent years. Vincent credits the increasing technologization of the harvesting process, with machines rendering most human labour redundant. At the same time, Marlene and Joe Thomas from Lennox Island First Nation, point to cheaper sources of migrant labour from Mexico and other countries displacing the Mi'kmaq. Today, the most common reason to go to Maine is to shop in Bangor or Freeport.

The cake is called "Poor Man's Cake" because all ingredients are inexpensive and easy to source. The trick is the cake's consistency before the blueberries are added—if it's too thin, they will sink to the bottom. Instead of measuring, Anne sets ratios for quantities. For example, a teaspoon of baking powder for each cup of flour, one part sugar to two parts flour, and water added gradually until reaching her desired consistency. Here is her recipe with our attempt to provide measurements.

Blueberry Cake ("Poor Man's Cake") RECITE

Yields 8–12 squares
Preparation time:
1 hour, 20 minutes
- -

Preheat oven to 350°F (175°C) and grease a 13- x 8-inch (33- x 20-cm) pan with margarine or butter.

In a medium bowl, cream margarine or butter with sugar and stir in lemon extract or zest.

Beat eggs separately and add to the mixture.

In another bowl, combine flour, baking powder, and salt.

Fold dry ingredients into wet ingredients gradually, alternating with water or milk. Mix thoroughly until there are no lumps. The batter should be thick enough to stick to the back of a wooden spoon.

Stir in blueberries, pour mixture into the pan, and bake for 65 minutes, or until a toothpick inserted in the middle comes out dry. Let cool, cut into squares, and serve with jam, blueberry coulis, whipped cream, or ice cream.

1/2 cup (125 ml) margarine or butter
1 cup (250 ml) sugar
1 tsp (5 ml) lemon extract or lemon zest
2 eggs
2 cups (500 ml) flour
2 tsp (10 ml) baking powder
1 tsp (5 ml) salt
2/3 cup (150 ml) water or milk
1 cup (250 ml) fresh or frozen blueberries

A variation for this recipe is **Gail Barlow's Upside-Down Cake** recipe, which she learned from Mi'giju' Barlow. You can use any fruit, but she reaches for fresh raspberries when they are in season.

Line a square cake pan with parchment, place a generous layer of fresh raspberries in the pan, three berries deep, ensuring they are evenly spread with no gaps between them. Sprinkle with sugar, and then add Anne's Poor Man's Cake batter (without the blueberries) on top.

After baking, let cool and then invert the pan onto a cutting board or serving platter, and peel back the parchment to reveal a colourful and tempting upside-down cake. Serve while still warm with ice cream.

Sponge Cake

Linda Sock

At the heart of many scrumptious cakes is a solid crumb recipe of readily available staple ingredients. Access to these ingredients was more difficult in the past, whereas today knowledge is lacking about how to make a cake's foundation.

When Linda Sock related her recipe for Sponge Cake, which she taught herself, she noted that younger generations seem to have stopped baking, even though there's nothing more convenient than a cake made to order in one's own kitchen! Born in Sipekne'katik (Indian Brook) First Nation, Nova Scotia, Linda was raised by her Mi'giju' Mary Julian Cabot in Shubenacadie from the age of five. While the rest of her siblings went to Shubenacadie Indian Residential School, Linda stayed home and learned to cook everything, from stews to cakes, beside her Mi'giju' on their wood stove.

Eels? I like them if nobody tells me what they are! –Linda Sock

Without a fridge and electricity, staples were stored in the cupboard, and strawberries and blueberries were available seasonally. Linda and her family picked blueberries and then potatoes (tapitatk) in Maine in the late summer and fall so that Mi'giju' could make pies and cakes. In Elsipogtog, and elsewhere in Mi'kma'ki, people living on reserve received rations directly from the Indian Agent of flour, butter, sugar, lard, eggs, and other sundries, or they used credit from the Indian Agent's store to procure these items. Some kept their own cows, pigs, and chickens to produce and trade eggs, milk, and butter for other items.

The ingredients for this cake represent, on one hand, the ways families meet over dishes that entice us to share and enjoy them together—a great reason to make it. On the other hand, these ingredients remind us of the troubled legacy that colonialism has left on families—what they eat, and how those ingredients are sourced.

This cake tastes great on its own, or served with blueberries, strawberries, and sweetened cranberries, or finished with a decadent icing to celebrate special occasions.

Sponge Cake RECIPE

Yields 8–12 squares
Preparation time:
1 hour, 10 minutes

Preheat oven to 350°F (175°C). Grease a 13- x 9-inch (33- x 23-cm) pan with butter or shortening and then dust with flour.

Mix dry ingredients together and set aside.

In a separate bowl, mix wet ingredients, and then incorporate them into the dry mixture. Mix everything for 2 minutes on medium speed until a thick, smooth batter forms.

Pour batter into the prepared pan. Bake in the centre of the oven for 45 minutes until evenly golden and a toothpick inserted into the centre comes out clean. Let cake cool for 10 minutes in the pan, then invert it on a wire rack to cool completely.

1 cup (250 ml) sugar
2 cups (500 ml) flour
1/2 tsp (2 ml) salt
3 tsp (15 ml) baking powder
2 eggs
1 tsp (5 ml) vanilla
1/2 cup (125 ml) butter, margarine, or shortening
1 cup (250 ml) milk

Store-bought **whipped creams** usually have a lot of sugar and preservatives. For a healthier option, whip some up at home with 35% whole cream using a whisk or mixer. Pour cream into a deep bowl so that any splatter will be contained. If desired, add 1 tsp (5 ml) vanilla and 1–2 tbsp (15–30 ml) maple syrup. Beat with a mixer for 2–3 minutes until the cream thickens and reaches the desired consistency. This will probably take 5 or more minutes longer with a whisk, so be patient and keep at it! Serve with strawberries or berries of your choice and enjoy.

Stuffed Salmon

Edward Peterpaul

The Richibucto River once teemed with so much salmon you could catch them from your boat by just extending a net over the water.

Herman and Freda May Simon (Augustine), along with their brother, found this out the hard way. They brought their net down to the shore along the river, and they could see the fish moving as if a great tide was approaching. So, they took a vote and decided to disobey their father by using their net to catch a fish. They were too little to carry a salmon very far, which is why their father told them not to use their net during spawning season. Sure enough, a salmon ends up in their net the moment the net enters the water. The three siblings struggled to draw it toward them back to shore and carried it clumsily back to their home in Elsipogtog.

Edward Peterpaul remembers fishing for salmon with his family and dog on Indian Island (the island that faces the reserve today). His grandfather set up a net in the water to catch their dinner, and his grandmother dug a one-foot-deep hole in the sand and lined it with rocks, while Edward and the other kids sourced material to build a large fire. Once the rocks grew red, his grandmother lined the bottom with sea sage that still grows along the shores of Rexton and Richibucto. After a freshly caught salmon was cleaned, she would stuff it with quahogs caught at low tide not far from the fire and season it with salt that she carried in a bag (witjiboti) strapped to her hip—where she also kept her pipe, matches, tobacco, flour, and baking powder. Then, she would cover the salmon with more sea sage.

Once the salmon is cooking, other components are layered on top, perhaps slices of potatoes, or Lu'sknikn that Edward's grandmother whipped up beside the fire. She placed sea sage between each layer, infusing everything with a flavour reminiscent of sea salt. She covered the Lu'sknikn with a pot lid to help contain the heat. When the dough was golden brown, several hours later, the meal was ready—just in time for dinner. Sand can be used to cover the dish while it cooks, rather than a pot lid. Just cover the top layer with sea sage and pack sand around the top so that it seals in the heat, placing wood on top to help keep the fire insulated.

It was my job to carry the rations home from the Indian Agent in Rexton, so about fifteen kilometres away from here. I was crying because that included a big bag of flour, maybe ten kilos. They gave us a gallon of molasses, plus five pounds of lard and a pound of sugar. It's not much, and that's all they gave us, but it sure felt like a lot to carry home to Big Cove!
—Edward Peterpaul

Edward seasons his salmon with salt pork instead of sea sage. When used for seasoning, there's no need to desalinate the salt pork. Edward also adds texture to the clam stuffing by incorporating crushed Ritz crackers as well as some aromatics.

> **Sea sage**, also known as saltbush, is high in protein and imparts a salty flavour to food, making it an ideal seasoning or to envelop fish for baking and roasting. You can find it along the shores of New Brunswick's east coast.

Edward's stuffed salmon fresh from the oven.

Stuffed Salmon RECIPE

Serves 4
Preparation time:
1 hour

- -

2 slices salt pork,
   trimmed of skin
   and cubed
1 box Ritz crackers,
   crushed
1 small can clams
1 small onion, diced
1 stalk celery, diced
1 whole salmon,
   1 1/2 lb (675 g),
   cleaned

Preheat oven to 350°F (175°C).

In a bowl, mix salt pork, crackers, clams (and any juice), onion, and celery, and stuff the salmon belly. Use a trussing needle and kitchen cotton twine to sew the belly closed.

Place trussed salmon on a rack in a casserole dish, cover with foil, and bake for 25 minutes.

Remove foil and baste with pan juices, and return to the oven uncovered for another 20 minutes, longer if salmon is large. Continue basting every few minutes until skin browns.

Serve with steamed fiddleheads, boiled potatoes, Chow Chow (see p. 62), and Lu'sknikn (see p. 99).

Fiddleheads can be steamed, deep-fried, or even roasted, but they can also be seasoned with pork belly. Brown pork belly cubes in a frying pan and then pour an inch or two of water into the pan, scraping off any brown bits from the bottom; add cleaned fiddleheads. Sauté for ten to fifteen minutes, adding more water as necessary, until the fiddleheads grow soft, and serve with the pork cubes. The salt and oil from the meat will deliciously coat and season the fiddleheads.

Salmon Stew

Gail Barlow

In memory of Mi'giju' Laura Barlow, the original contributor of the recipe.

A tail section of Atlantic salmon.

Atlantic salmon is a valuable fish across the world. Overfishing has meant less availability and low quotas, resulting in fish farming operations. Salmon served raw to rare in sushi, tartare, and similar dishes, is high in several types of vitamin B and omega-3s. If you prefer it cooked—fried, grilled, roasted, steamed, or stewed—you will still benefit from this rich source of protein that is low in calories.

The colour of salmon flesh gives any dish vibrancy. This salmon stew draws its flavour from the bones and skin of the fish, while the tasty fat that often gets discarded on the inside facing of the skin melts into the soup, giving it unexpected depth of flavour. This recipe can be made with mackerel in the fall when it is in season.

We have an important advantage in this region: pretty much everything comes fresh out of the water so you don't have to do a lot to it to make a marvellous meal, and you can use traditional methods to store it to use in other times of the year. –Gail Barlow

- -

1 1/2 lb (675 g) whole
  salmon, cleaned,
  cut into 8–10
  sections, skin and
  bones intact
salt and pepper, to
  taste
1 large onion, peeled
  and cut in half
4 large potatoes,
  peeled and cut
  into 1-inch cubes
1 large carrot, finely
  diced
1 celery stick, sliced
  into small pieces
1 tbsp (15 ml) butter

For dumplings
1 cup (250 ml) flour
1/2 tsp (2 ml) salt
1 tsp (5 ml) baking
  powder
1/4 cup (60 ml) cold
  water

Salmon Stew RECIPE

In a pot, submerge salmon in cold water so that it is just covered, and add salt. Bring to a boil, then cover, and let simmer on medium heat for 20 minutes.

Remove fish and place on a cutting board, but do not drain the water as this will be our broth for the stock.

Remove bones and skin from fish, and then break its meat into spoon-size pieces and set aside. Don't worry if some salmon is not yet cooked—it will complete cooking during the next step. Discard bones and skin.

Place onion halves, potatoes, carrot, celery, butter, cooked salmon, and pepper in cooking water. Cook covered until potatoes are tender, about 25 minutes.

Meanwhile, prepare dumplings by mixing flour with salt and baking powder in a bowl. Make a well in the middle and slowly pour in cold water.

Using a wooden spoon or your hands, bring dough together into one large ball. Sprinkle in more flour if it is too sticky.

Shape into 12 balls using a tablespoon and as you form each, add to the stew. Once all balls have been added, cover, and cook for 10 minutes without removing the lid.

Serve with Lu'sknikn (see p. 99), Pipnaqn or rolls (see p. 110), and Chow Chow (see p. 62).

Laura Barlow was an Elder born in Metepenagiag First Nation and grew up in Esgenoopetitj First Nation (meaning "lookout point"). She and her husband, Chief Peter J. Barlow, raised a large family in Indian Island First Nation. Laura was a remarkable cook. Her granddaughter, Tara Barlow, remembers that her Mi'giju' Laura "fed the world...every child, wandering man, lost animal. She made a home for everyone."

Gail Barlow's loose recipe container.

Gail Barlow moved to Indian Island First Nation from Metepenagiag First Nation as a young woman. In both communities, she says, "there is always a time for things." In spring and early summer, the first treat that presents itself is wild strawberries. For the rest of the summer, blueberries, blackberries, and raspberries are plentiful. Everybody knows the cycle of nature's bounty and traditionally Mi'kmaq children learn to seek it out. Gail shares that "as children, we would go up the hill to see if the blueberries were ready to pick. We'd snack on them, but we were mostly gathering them to bring them home so that my mother would make even better dishes with them—blueberry cake, blueberry pie—or she'd freeze them for the winter."

Nijinjk (Salmon Roe)
Anita Joseph

M ost people have heard of caviar or fish roe. These eggs are harvested from the ovaries of cold-water fish, including salmon, trout, and beluga sturgeon. They are eaten raw as an accompaniment or condiment and are considered a rare luxury ingredient. Each egg resembles a colourful pearl that has been brined or salted, resulting in a concentrated and salty flavour, with bursting juiciness, that pleases the palate.

For the following recipe, the eggs are left in the membrane once it is harvested from the salmon so that they stay together, making the

The trick to cooking wild game so to balance out the flavour and ensure it's tender, is to marinate it in something acidic—vinegar, soda, wine—whatever you have on hand. –Anita Joseph

Anita sometimes serves this dish chilled as an **appetizer** using crackers in a way that resembles how caviar is consumed. These hors d'oeuvres can be accompanied by capers, a sprig of dill, and Chow Chow (p. 62) or a sliver of preserved lemon.

texture of this dish quite different from a typical caviar—or a roasted salmon loin, or tail steak. Baked salmon roe is usually served as a side dish with salad or potatoes or alongside an entrée of roasted salmon. Like caviar, it is considered a treat.

This cut of the salmon is difficult to procure. Atlantic wild salmon fishers do not usually harvest the head and the ovaries, as opposed to fish grown specifically for their eggs to be sold as caviar, so Anita asks local fishers to keep the roe for her. Herman J. Simon and his sister Freda May Augustine remember how their father would preserve salmon and the eggs in a barrel with salt (alongside barrels for herring and other fish).

Anita Joseph comes from a long line of fishers, and growing up she ate baked salmon roe at least once a week. Although she also enjoys roe during the summer, the best time to harvest it is in the fall when the salmon spawn. Her family would freeze the roe to eat throughout the year. At that time, there was such an abundance of salmon in the Richibucto River that her Uncle Hubert would come back with five fish each time he went fishing for his family's dinner. Now, John Levi and other local fishers bring her salmon and make sure that the roe is intact to use in dishes like this one.

Nijinjk (Salmon Roe) RECIPE

Preheat the oven to 250°F (120°C).

Place salmon eggs in a greased casserole dish. Gently pour water into the bottom of the dish and sprinkle salmon with salt and pepper.

Spread butter along the top of the eggs and then layer onion on top of the salmon.

Cover the casserole dish with foil or a lid and bake for 2 hours.

Serve chilled as a side with fresh tomatoes and cucumbers, or warm with roasted salmon, potatoes, and vegetables.

Serves 4
Preparation time:
2 hours, 10 minutes

- -

1/2 lb (225 g) fresh or frozen salmon eggs or roe (nijinjk)
3/4 cup (175 ml) water
salt and pepper, to taste
1 tbsp (15 ml) softened butter
1 small onion, sliced into rings

Traditionally, the **Mi'kmaq eat all parts of the animal** or find other uses for it so that nothing goes to waste—whether that's by drying deer hide to make bags or clothing, harvesting porcupine quills for regalia and the decorative arts, conserving rabbit's blood for stews, boiling the bones for a soup stock, and preparing salmon eggs for baked or boiled roe.

Lobster Subs

John Levi and Toby Augustine

In loving memory of John Levi. He and his wife gifted us this recipe. John, who was a War Chief, led the fight against fracking in New Brunswick. He passed away in 2023.

Toby Augustine and John Levi.

Between our hunters and fishers, we can feed the entire community. –John Levi

Born in 1968, John Levi was raised by his parents in Elsipogtog along with six siblings and about eight cousins. Like his siblings, he is also known by another name—John Katew (eel) because he was born in May during eel season. His brother is Robert Wapus (rabbit) because he was born in January during rabbit-hunting season. Three members of his family are called Peju because they were born during cod-fishing season. This naming practice reinforces how Mi'kmaw identity is inherently linked to local ingredients, traditional ecological knowledge, and how the region experiences the seasons.

Lobster has been transformed in the last century or so into a luxury commodity on the global market, which also impacted the Atlantic fisheries. Before settlers came, the Mi'kmaq ate lobster and used the shells for decorative arts. They hunted lobster along the shore using a spear or a

John's parents had their challenges, but the way they faced them helped to shape him into a role model for the community. His mother, like her siblings, was taken to the Shubenacadie Indian Residential School. She didn't talk about it much; she devoted her life to raising John and the young ones in the family. She was known most famously for her creative approach to making the best of what was in the cupboard. John's father was a year-round fisher who brought home whatever was in season—salmon, bass, eels. When John's father was a young man, John's grandfather was injured in the potato house in Maine and remained disabled for the rest of his life. John's father stepped in as the family's provider, and then John became a provider for his community.

sharp stick at low tide, which would be roasted and then consumed. Today, lobster traps and specialized equipment are used for the harvest, usually off the coast in deeper water.

Mi'kmaq fishers exercise their treaty rights, which date back to the eighteenth-century Peace and Friendship Treaties (i.e., 1726, 1752, and 1760-1761) in which sovereignty, hunting and fishing rights, and trading rights were agreed upon. Unfortunately, they have been persecuted for exercising their treaty rights, challenged when they fail to produce government-granted fishing licenses, and fined when they sell fish to support their families. In 1999, the Supreme Court of Canada recognized Mi'kmaq fishers' treaty right to hunt and earn a "moderate livelihood" in what is known as the Marshall Decision, named after Donald Marshall Jr. who brought the matter to the country's highest court.

Many Canadians misunderstand these decisions and the scope of Indigenous rights. Perhaps some only see lobster as a commodity on the global market. Others might not realize that the entire harvest does not go to the commercial market to help a fisher earn a modest livelihood. Rather, it is given in generous quantities to help sustain and nourish their community while ensuring that fishing practices are sustainable. These foods are also harvested for ceremonies to reinforce the Mi'kmaq's connection to the land and water. Lobster, moose, salmon—whatever the hunter brings to the community—represent a significant equalizer. Regardless of one's

A **War Chief**, and warriors in general, fights to defend the community's interests. When Elders appointed John War Chief several years ago, one of his first challenges was New Brunswick's commercial exploration of fracking—a process through which gas or oil is extracted from deep in the earth using destructive forces that can have grave environmental consequences. The community's main concern was how fracking would affect water quality, as water is everything—it nourishes not only Elsipogtog and the surrounding region, but it also gives life to the fish and land-based food. As John pointed out, "When the water's gone, what are we going to do? It's not like we will move on and find a new home. Traditionally, we come back to the same places."

Settlers, seeing how fracking would also impact their quality of life, joined the fight a few years ago. John organized the broader offensive against fracking, resulting in companies backing off in 2013. As a result of people like John, New Brunswick's water security is more protected now than if commercial interests had prevailed.

Serves 4–6
Preparation time:
1 hour, 10 minutes
to cook and clean
lobster, 25 minutes for
assembly

- -

For lobster
1/4 cup (60 ml) salt
6 medium-sized live
    lobster
1 bag of ice

For subs
4 leaves iceberg or
    romaine lettuce,
    chopped
1/2 cup (125 ml)
    mayonnaise
salt and pepper, to
    taste
1 tbsp (15 ml) butter
8–12 hot-dog buns

class, how much money they have to buy food, or where they live, freely given and healthy food embodies the Mi'kmaw philosophy of nurturing their community. It is also vital to point out that the scale of Indigenous fishing in the region is small compared to corporate fishing companies that are largely responsible for imperilling Atlantic stocks due to overfishing.

The lobster sub recipe John shares with us is more than a recipe. It represents an ongoing fight for rights. The amount of lobster is generous, bountiful on the plate, and satiating—the ultimate gift that a fisher bestows upon the hungry and eager recipient.

Whether you use live or cooked lobster, be sure to utilize the shells afterward. Prepare a stock by browning them in a deep pot with 1 tbsp (15 ml) butter or oil. Some people like to include onion, celery, and carrots. Pour in enough water to generously cover the shells and cover with a lid. Bring to a boil over high heat, then reduce to medium–low and leave to simmer for 30 minutes. Strain and refrigerate, or freeze the stock. It can be used for rice dishes, stews, and any seafood dish that requires liquid.

Lobster Subs RECIPE

Bring a large pot of water to a boil—this may take 30 minutes or more, so plan accordingly—and then place lobster in the pot and cover. Once the water returns to boil, reduce heat to medium-low and cook for 20–30 minutes, depending on size.

Remove lobster from the pot and place them in an ice bath in the sink so that they cool and stop cooking. This ensures that the lobster meat won't stick to the shell when they are cracked.

Using a lobster cracker or nutcracker, clean lobster from the shell and re-frigerate until ready to use. Be sure to squeeze meat out of the claws, tail, body, and legs. Reserve shells and remaining juices to make your lobster stock.

To assemble subs, roughly chop lobster into small pieces and place in a medium bowl. Add lettuce, mayonnaise, and salt and pepper, and mix lightly so that ingredients are evenly combined. Place in the fridge.

Melt butter in a medium-sized pan on medium heat. When butter turns golden brown, place buns in the pan and grill for three minutes on each

side. If you need to do this in batches, use more butter for each batch. When buns are toasted, place on serving plates and stuff with lobster mix. Serve immediately and enjoy!

I suggest mixing lettuce and lobster with mayonnaise for a seasonal sandwich in the summer. But hold the onions—they hide the wonderful flavour of the lobster.
–Toby Augustine

The Indian Agent and Rations

Today, "welfare" is synonymous with "rations" in communities such as Elsipogtog First Nation because, starting in the 1950s, a share of food was given to each family—a time when most of this cookbook's contributors grew up. It was similar to a gift certificate for a specified amount meant to be spent on food. Thursday is still referred to as "ration day" because this is the day government support payments are deposited to welfare recipients.

Many people remember Lee Fraser's role in their lives. As the Indian Agent stationed in Rexton, New Brunswick, he was employed by the government to administer the Indian Act in the area. He also ran the local market and gave families rations, while he sold his other groceries at a premium. The Indian Act is a powerful document introduced by the Canadian government in 1876 that defines who is Indigenous and what their rights are, including what sorts of support settler governments owe the Mi'kmaq. Over the decades it has been broadly criticized for how it disenfranchises women and children from their Indigenous identity, and how it constrains the Mi'kmaq's relationship with their traditional foodways. The Indian Agent had wide-ranging influence over Mi'kmaq lives—he could even split up children and send them to different schools, hundreds of kilometres away from their communities, as far away as Moncton and Fredericton.

Rations typically included foods beyond what the Mi'kmaq could grow—flour, sugar, tea leaves, molasses, and sometimes lard. A family's allocation was predetermined and documented by the Indian Agent. If you needed more, you had to pay cash. Anne Barlow remembers non-perishable items also distributed by the Indian Agent. Each fall, he would drop off a bundle of gum rubbers—a rubber covering that is pulled over one's shoes to the ankles to keep them dry—at the school for students, as well as toothbrushes and toothpaste.

Because the store was located across the Richibucto River in Rexton, several kilometres away, community members had to use a boat or, in the winter months after the river had frozen, a horse and buggy or sleigh over the ice. Many, however, didn't even have access to transportation.

In Elsipogtog, little stores operated by people like George Peterpaul were designated by Indian Affairs to be outlets where one could buy a variety of items—dried beans for baked beans, yeast for bread, chicken for dinner (which in the Maritimes usually refers to lunch rather than supper), and butter for people who didn't have cows. Sometimes settlers squatted in communities—Gail Barlow recalls this in Metepenagiag (Red Bank) when she was growing up—where they sold foods beyond rations at a good profit by allowing people to open accounts and pay later.

With such large families—often ten to fifteen mouths to feed—the cost of food became a significant factor in a family's quality of life. As Gail points out, between rations and the government's infringement on their treaty rights to limit their ability to hunt and fish, the attempt to wipe out the Mi'kmaq can be fundamentally traced to this genocidal and deliberate manipulation of their foodways. The end of the consumption of traditional moose, deer, and even lobster, dovetailed with the turn away from the seasonal and local fruits and vegetables upon which the Mi'kmaq had relied for ages and toward cheap, carbohydrate-rich food like macaroni, doughnuts, and other sugary replacements. The Mi'kmaq now wouldn't need to leave the reserves and interact with the settlers, or suffer harassment while hunting and fishing outside the already-small reserve boundaries.

At the same time, government resistance to expanding reserves to allow more sustainable food and income streams has meant that places like Elsipogtog, for example, have sacrificed forest where people would hunt, or land to grow food, in order to build houses. There is a housing crisis on many reserves in the country, as Indigenous Peoples are the fastest-growing demographic in Canada. Since the creation of Elsipogtog in 1805, the size has shrunk and now equals one-third of its original footprint. (Elsipogtog and its members also have reserves in Moncton and other areas of the province.)

The Indian Agent did not give out other meats that could be hunted on the reserve or on Crown lands, or fish from the region's rivers and the ocean, as per the Mi'kmaq's established treaty rights. As explored throughout this cookbook, exercising one's treaty rights has its challenges, even today. Furthermore, some reserves—Indian Island, for example, almost entirely surrounded by water—have few hunting grounds, so this compels people to either travel to hunt, or to compromise and purchase what they need from a nearby supermarket or store.

The Mi'kmaq always find ways to make use of everything, and ration containers were no different. Flour bags, for example, would be sewn together and turned into a quilt backing. The material was also useful to be transformed into diapers for families with infants.

Fall

Elder Gary Joe Augustine from Elsipogtog is a basket maker and builds traditional wigwams and longhouses.

The Story of Selling Baskets in Moncton

From a young age, children like eight-year-old Ashley learned to weave small baskets. Some are practical—a basket for picking potatoes with a sling for the shoulder or a basket for toothbrushes hanging in the bathroom—whereas others are fancy and decorative, and even thematically decorated to suit the product they were intended to carry.

Like raking blueberries and picking potatoes in Maine, selling baskets was a significant means for Ashley's family to earn money, which they needed to procure items they couldn't grow or hunt, or that couldn't be obtained by trade—textiles for clothing, as well as shoes. Historically, baskets were a necessity for cooking, gardening, and for food storage. Until recent years, people all over the Maritimes needed a range of baskets, and the Mi'kmaq have proven themselves to be expert basket makers.

Ashley's family lived in a house in Elsipogtog with an open kitchen, dining, and living area where they made baskets and related products, including chairs woven from flexible varieties of wood, and hammer and axe handles, which they sold in nearby towns and in Moncton. The material of choice—black ash and maple—is scarce today, but was readily accessible not long ago. As a result, Ashley's baskets were always a wood shade of white, which allowed them to be dramatically transformed when her father dyed them the vibrant colours their customers eagerly desired.

Parents, especially fathers and grandfathers, would go into the woods towing a sled and collect ash. They'd pull what they found back home and load it into the house where the family worked the wood into baskets, handles—whatever they were practiced at. From September to December, Ashley and her siblings went into the woods to collect conifer branches which they wove into round wreaths and decorated with berries.

It was the second week of December, 1956, and downtown Moncton was humming with Christmas shoppers, friends, and neighbours cheerfully greeting each other, and the Mi'kmaq families who went there to sell baskets and wreaths. Ashley and her mother had brought ninety-six wreaths and one hundred and three baskets of various sizes to sell over the next couple of days.

Ashley thought Moncton was the most interesting place, especially with the big city's strange smells. It was late afternoon; the sky was darkening and the lights emanating from shop windows sparkled. Standing on a snow-covered Main Street sidewalk facing in the direction of the train station from which she and her mother had just emerged, she looked at the people hurrying to and fro around her. She was in charge of speaking to potential customers, as her mother didn't know much English. While some of her friends' families came to Moncton by horse and wagon, her family didn't have a horse, so they caught the train from the Saint-Charles stop near Elsipogtog that morning, which brought them to Moncton in time to sell a few baskets and wreaths that afternoon.

She lamented not being able to carry more than two or three baskets and wreaths at a time, especially because many of their sales came from knocking on residential and commercial doors—the bread and butter of their trade. But her mother was laden with baskets as she tied them to a sack she carried on her back. They bounced around her as they made their way around the centre of the city, walking down one residential street in the direction of the Moncton Hospital before darting over to the next street and weaving back toward the downtown, knocking on doors as they went. The rest of the wreaths and baskets were stored in a locker they rented at the train station. They took only what they thought would sell that day, and returned to the station to retrieve more as necessary.

While Ashley loved the way the setting sun brought the Petitcodiac River alive with twinkles and sparkling ice crystals, she much preferred the summer months when her family camped on Cape Breton Road in Irishtown. There, they set up a wigwam or tarpaper shack along the railway and could hop on the train to sell baskets in town and then return to rest for the night. Ash was also plentiful in the area, so her family sometimes stayed for days at a time, alternating between making baskets at camp and selling them in town. The conductor would slow down if he saw a Mi'kmaw near the tracks because he knew that they were coming to Moncton. Ashley loved chasing after the train and clambering into the railcar. They didn't have to pay for transportation into the city, but they had to stay in the cargo compartment and couldn't sit with the other passengers.

That chilly night, though, Ashley knew they'd be staying in Moncton. The police station in the city's downtown offered lodging, and many Indigenous women and their children would sleep on the second floor, which at that time was one large, empty room lined with warm radiators, except for a cell in the middle where an occasional prisoner was kept. Ashley loved it here because the radiators and rustling of other families made the night so cozy. She also enjoyed pretending not to know English whenever a prisoner would try to speak with her. The next morning, they gave her and her mother a breakfast of bread, jam, and tea, and then they set out for their next day of trading.

The first day was good as they sold fifty-seven wreaths and forty-nine baskets. On their second day, they sold all their wares, and Ashley's mother took her to Eaton's and bought her a pair of shiny black shoes for her first Communion. They cost $2—half the amount they had made from their sales that trip. Then they went across the parking lot to catch the next train home.

Elder Gary Joe Augustine explains the basket-making process to Nimbus editor Whitney Moran in Elsipogtog.

Gaspalaw (Salted Herring) with Potatoes

Mary Irene Augustine

For most of us, potatoes (tapitatk) come from a bag purchased in a store or from a local farmers' market. Mary Irene remembers growing up with a garden beside her home in Elsipogtog. Her mother would always pick potatoes fresh from the garden when they have the best flavour and juiciness to make this recipe. Then she would unlock a shed where the family stored salt pork before continuing to yet another shed where salt herring and cod was stored. Many Mi'kmaq remember large barrels or sheds full of salted fish and meats to use throughout the year, each stored in its own container.

The root cellar wasn't just for root vegetables after the harvest, we also kept lettuce down there. I used to sneak down there, take some lettuce, wash it, and come up to share it with my brother!
–Mary Irene Augustine

Mary Irene's father salted the pork and fish in her family. Salting fish has traditionally been an important means of preserving food. Today, most of us purchase fish already salted—salt cod and salt herring among the most popular—and after we bring it home, we soak it in water for one to two days, changing the water a few times. Another option for desalinating fish is to boil it to accelerate the process. Mary Irene's recipe combines both methods, which has the added benefit of producing herring that is hot and ready to eat.

Desalinating the fish washes away most of the salt, leaving a texture between raw and cooked. It's edible as is and can be incorporated into various dishes, from fish cakes and croquettes to casseroles and salads.

The **salt pork** used in this dish traditionally has other purposes beyond nourishment and seasoning—it is also a trusted medicine. Anita Joseph recalls how she used to take a thin slice of salt pork, place it on a small cut or a minor infection, cover with a bandage, and by the next day the inflammation or infection had improved.

Before using the desalinated fish, however, be sure to check for bones. As mentioned earlier, salt pork doesn't need to be soaked when used as a seasoning—it is added to a dish after dicing or frying it to impart flavour. Sometimes, however, it is boiled or stewed before serving to reduce its salt content and soften its texture.

While Mi'kmaq families harvested potatoes in Maine each fall, some chose to live there year-round to work in processing and shipping potatoes throughout the continent after the fall harvest. Jake Sock remembers growing up with his parents in Maine before moving to Elsipogtog. As a young man, he returned there to work for a potato farmer full time. His employer also provided a house where he eventually lived with his long-time wife, Geraldine.

While this recipe calls for salted herring, salt cod and salt mackerel will also work well and bring different fish flavours to the dish.

Gaspalaw with Potatoes RECIPE

Soak herring overnight in water, changing water once or twice. Rinse several times in cool water, then place fish in a pot covered with water.

In a second pot, place potatoes in a pot covered in water. Bring both pots to a boil, then reduce to medium heat for 25 minutes until potatoes are tender when pricked with a fork.

While herring and potatoes cook, heat oil in a frying pan on medium-high heat, and fry salted pork until brown.

Drain herring and potatoes, and arrange on a platter so that herring is covered by potatoes. Top with onion. Sprinkle the dish with salt pork, using any remaining drippings from the pan as dressing. Serve while warm.

Serves 4
Preparation time:
35 minutes

- -

4 pieces (1–1 1/2 lbs, 450–675 g) salted herring
4 large potatoes, peeled and quartered
2 tbsp (30 ml) oil
1 onion, sliced
1 lb (450 g) salted pork, finely cubed

Apple Pie
Georgina Barlow

Growing up there was always a pot of stew on the stove, and guests—whether from the community or people from Indian Affairs—would sit around the table and eat Mum's stew.—Georgina Barlow

Like flour, apples were imported to present-day Atlantic Canada by French settlers, first in Nova Scotia's Annapolis Valley in the 1630s. From there cultivation spread. And today Nova Scotia exports more apples than any other province. While we eat apples as a snack, or use them as the focus of recipes like Georgina's pie, in the past apples were fermented to produce a cider imbibed instead of wine and other alcohol that was difficult for settlers to make. New varieties of apples were engineered to withstand the cold. The Mi'kmaw relationship with the apple can be traced back to their labour in both an Indigenous and settler context. Mi'kmaq workers

harvested apples in New Brunswick starting about two hundred years ago. They also crafted the baskets to collect the fruit—an Indigenous innovation. Apples are cultivated using methods that reflect other settler-colonial crops, such that land used for hunting and gathering among the Mi'kmaq was converted into purpose-built orchards. People throughout the area, including Indian Island, harvest apples each fall just after the first frost.

The Barlow family from Indian Island First Nation. Sitting: Gertrude Nicholas Barlow; her dad, Chief Peter Barlow; her mum, Mrs, Laura Barlow; her sister Patsy Barlow. Standing: Gertrude's brother Raymond Garfield Barlow; her sister Loretta Nicholas Barlow; other brother, Second Peter Barlow.

In this way, community members have continued over the generations to make the best of what resources lie at their fingertips, even when those resources do not originate from their traditional territory. Instead of blueberries that once grew in a clearing, today an orchard provides the community with an alternative, nutritious food source. But, from another perspective, pressure from settler-colonial authorities over the centuries has meant that crops alien to the traditional Mi'kmaw culinary world often don't get harvested, which has sometimes led to people being incorrectly stereotyped as lazy. These practices support a broader effort to maintain the non-human world. Unharvested fruit falls to the ground and nourishes a local ecosystem, which includes bears, foxes, and deer. Ecological steward-ship, which informs a broadly held worldview throughout the Indigenous world of "all my relations," should give us all pause the next time we find ourselves under an apple tree in Sikniktuk. There is a reason why some apples get picked and others remain.

When Linda Sock and other community members remember picking apples as a child, they recognize that their mothers and grandmothers always knew where and when to pick the best apples, as if a culinary map unfolded each season and everyone knew where to go for the freshest fruit. Linda confesses, however, that while picking apples, her motivation was always what would become of them once her grandmother had them safely back in their family kitchen!

Sometimes, **pie crusts** can be mushy rather than flaky. Georgina suggests using greased aluminum pie plates because the aluminum reflects the heat, which will help set the pie's bottom crust and give it colour, while improving the crust's flavour.

Apple Pie RECIPE

Yields 3 pies
Preparation time:
2 hours

5 cups (1.1 L) flour
pinch salt
1 tsp (5 ml) baking
powder
1 lb (450 g) lard,
chilled
1 egg yolk
1 tbsp (15 ml) vinegar
1 cup (250 ml) cold
water, plus more as
needed
5-lb (2-kg) bag
apples, preferably
a combination
of McIntosh and
Cortland
1/3 cup (79 ml) sugar
3 tsp (15 ml) ground
cinnamon
1 tbsp (15 ml) butter,
softened
1 egg (plus more for
coating the top
crust; optional)

Preheat the oven to 350°F (175°C).

In a large bowl, mix flour, salt, and baking powder. Cut lard into slices, then mix it into flour mixture using two butter knives, or even a sturdy whisk until the largest pieces are the size of peas.

In a measuring cup, use a fork to combine egg yolk and vinegar, then pour in cold water. Whisk gently using a fork.

Incorporate the wet mixture into the dry mixture until evenly combined. Add more cold water if necessary to form the dough into a ball. Be careful not to overmix.

Turn onto a floured surface, cut into 6 pieces, and form into balls. Then place in a bowl and cover. Allow dough to chill in the fridge for at least 30 minutes before rolling.

In the meantime, ready your filling ingredients by peeling and slicing apples.

On a floured surface, use a floured rolling pin to roll one dough ball into a round slightly larger than the pie pan; this will be the base. Roll the round over the rolling pin and gently place into the pie dish.

Place a layer of apples on the bottom crust. Sprinkle 2 tbsp (30 ml) sugar and 1/3 tsp (1.5 ml) cinnamon over the layer, and then place two more layers of apples, each time seasoning with the same amount of sugar and cinnamon. If you prefer your pie sweeter, sprinkle a bit more sugar at each stage of the layering. Dot butter on top.

Repeat these steps for the other two pies.

Then roll out a second ball for the top of each pie and place the second pie crust over each mixture.

Trim any excess dough and then seal the two crusts by dampening the bottom edge of the pie crust with a little bit of water while using your fingers or a fork to pinch or gather them together to form pleats.

Cut three slits on each pie crust to let the steam vent during cooking. Then, sprinkle 1 tbsp (15 ml) sugar on each and gently press it in the dough with your hands.

To make egg wash, whisk an egg with 1 tbsp (15 ml) water and brush the pies just before putting them in the oven. Bake for 1 hour in the middle of the oven.

Apple pie is dressed differently depending on the community in which you find yourself. In Elsipogtog, it is accompanied by ice cream, whereas in Indian Island it is also served with cheddar cheese.

Swiss Steak with Moose Meat

Lulu Sock

Growing up in Elsipogtog First Nation, Lulu Sock remembers how her father hunted moose, duck, and rabbit, and her grandmother would prepare stews. At that age, she wasn't a fan of the taste of wild game, but over the years it became a comfort from her childhood. The rabbits would be strung up along the ceiling of the covered porch during the winter and brought inside to thaw when they were needed for dinner. Lulu's mother died when she was young, so she learned to cook from her grandmother while her father worked for a woodworking company. He had lost his arm there, but despite his disability, he hunted alongside her grandfather on his day off each week, bringing home a variety of meats, even moose.

Swiss steak is a meal many families would eat throughout the week, popular because it made use of cheaper or undesirable cuts of meat. The cooking process helps to soften the meat, making it easier to consume while providing a sauce that gives the meat richer flavour. Some people would start it in the morning using a slow cooker so that it would be ready later in the day for supper. While some might associate it with Switzerland, the dish is actually named after the "swissing" technique used to tenderize meat—even large cuts—by pounding, or in this case, by braising it in sauce. Lulu's recipe asks for a moose roast, but you can source the loin or other larger cuts—or substitute beef.

Onion flakes and celery seeds can certainly be substituted with minced fresh onion and celery. You can prepare this dish as Lulu does on the stovetop or in a casserole dish in an oven preheated to 350°F (175°C).

We never had powwows growing up. Instead, every summer, people would come for two to three days of picnic and dancing during the Ste. Anne celebration in July. People would come on foot, on horse, in cars, and a lot of people came along the shore in their boats, and they'd camp in the community. –Lulu Sock

Lulu Sock's meat mixture ready for braising.

Geraldine Sock and Gordon Francis grew up eating fish and wild game. Gordon remembers the first time he tried beef: "It was too bland to me because the wild, gamey taste was missing, and I didn't really like it. The texture was fine, but the flavour was off-putting. After we got welfare, we started eating beef and pork regularly, and the blandness became normal. A few years ago, I went back to eating moose and deer again, and the gamey taste was overwhelming at first. So, it took me a while to get back into the groove and eat game again, but now I love the taste of moose."

Serves 4–6
Preparation time:
2 hours, plus time to
marinate the meat.

For marinade
¼ cup (60 ml) vinegar
2 tbsp (30 ml) water
2/3 cup (150 ml) oil
1/2 tsp (2 ml) dry
     mustard
1 tsp (5 ml) salt
1 tbsp (15 ml) ketchup
1 tbsp (15 ml) grated
     onion or dried
     onion flakes
1/2 tsp (2 ml) sugar
1/4 tsp (1 ml) pepper
1/2 tsp (2 ml) paprika
1/4 tsp (1 ml) garlic
     salt

For moose steak
1 1/2 lb (675 g) round
     steak
1/4 cup flour (60 ml)
1/2 tsp (2 ml) salt
1/4 tsp (1 ml) pepper
4 tbsp (60 ml) oil
1 green pepper,
     halved and sliced
     (optional)
10–12 mushrooms,
     sliced (optional)
3 tbsp (45 ml) onion
     flakes

cont'd on 57

Swiss Steak with Moose Meat RECIPE

With a whisk, combine marinade ingredients in a bowl large enough to accommodate steak. Place steak in bowl and marinate overnight in the refrigerator.

The next day, remove steak from the marinade, trim excess fat, and wipe dry with a clean, damp cloth.

Combine flour, salt, and pepper, then dredge steak, shaking off any excess flour mixture.

Heat oil in a deep, thick-bottomed frying pan on high heat. Fry steak on all sides until brown, then remove to a plate.

If using green peppers and mushrooms, gently sauté in the same frying pan until their moisture releases. Add onion flakes, celery seed, tomatoes, and Worcestershire sauce, and stir until well mixed. Scrape off any brown bits stuck to the bottom of the pan to enhance the liquid's flavour. Bring to a low boil, then return steak to the pan, cover, reduce the heat to low, and simmer for 90 minutes.

Skodagon is a common accompaniment for roast moose or beef dinners. Lulu's cousin Marlene Thomas makes hers by mashing roasted potatoes and turnip with some gravy from the roast. If you roast the vegetables in the same pan as the meat, the drippings will already have permeated the vegetables, so you may only need to add a touch of butter and season to your taste before serving. Marlene's husband, Joe, likes to add carrots to his skodagon.

The word means "mixture of turnip and potato" in Mi'kmaw, and is adaptable as a side dish for chicken and gravy, and any meat dish with gravy, so it will pair well with Lulu Sock's Swiss steak.

Remove meat to a cutting board to rest. Make sauce by returning the pan to high heat so that mixture begins to boil. Prepare paste from remaining flour and water, and add it slowly, stirring constantly until liquid thickens into a gravy.

Thinly slice steak and serve with sauce accompanied by Four Cents (see p. 100), Lu'sknikn (see p. 99), or Pipnaqn (see p. 110).

cont'd from 56

1 tsp (5 ml) celery
  seed
2 cups (500 ml)
  canned tomatoes,
  diced
2 tbsp (30 ml)
  Worcestershire
  sauce
3 tbsp (45 ml) flour for
  thickening
1/2 cup (125 ml) cold
  water

Trinity and her brother Marshall Paquette cleaning a moose.

The Mi'kmaq today have protected hunting and fishing rights, although even those can be contested at times. But just a few decades ago, things weren't as straightforward. John Levi remembers how when he was little the Department of Natural Resources would harass Mi'kmaq hunters, telling them they couldn't hunt even on their own land. They did anyway, although with a touch of creativity.

One time, his uncle shot three moose across the river at Big Hill. Because of the prohibition on hunting, they didn't dare use the highway to transport the moose back to the community. His uncle mobilized twenty-five or so men to load each moose into a boat and crossed at night to Elsipogtog. They hung them in John's family's shed for a few days, after which they were ready to butcher. People came by the shed and John's uncle sliced off whatever amount and cut they desired.

Uncle Herman's Partridge Stew

Herman J. Simon

Herman John Simon with his sister Freda May Augustine shortly before his passing.

Go where the food is. –Herman J. Simon

Herman Simon passed away a few days after he shared this recipe with the help of his sister, Freda May Augustine. Despite living a block or so away from each other in Elsipogtog, mobility issues kept the two siblings from visiting as much as they would have liked. Freda May is now the sole surviving child of five boys and five girls in her family.

Their mother would prepare traditional sources of protein like rabbit and moose, along with other wild meats. The Mi'kmaq refer to grouse (plaqawej) as partridge in English. Herman and Freda May also ate the eggs of wild avian species, including both partridge and seagull. Seagull eggs are large, like those of a chicken, and Herman advised us when harvesting them from nests to never take more than one or two at a time. If there are more than two eggs in a nest, he counselled, that means they've been there for a while and might have a baby bird already developing, whereas if there are only one or two eggs, that means they've been freshly laid and are safe to eat. He also pointed out that it's important not to take all the eggs because the bird colony needs to survive as well.

Wild meats can have a taste that some people may find different. Mi'giju' Susie Ann had a lot of experience coming from a family of hunters with a constant supply of fresh meat. Her secret was to marinate moose, rabbit, or deer in baking soda and water overnight to tenderize it. She would also boil the meat with a few tablespoons of vinegar for half an hour before incorporating it into a casserole and baking for several hours.

Herman assured us that the following recipe can be used for either rabbit or partridge stew. It makes for an easy, one-pot meal that comes together quickly and doesn't require a lot of attention. If neither of these proteins are available, try it with chicken or turkey.

Uncle Herman's Partridge Stew RECIPE

Place all ingredients in a medium pot with water to cover. Put on a lid and bring the pot to a boil, then reduce to a slow simmer and cook for 1 hour. Season with salt and pepper.

Ladle partridge breast and vegetables into a bowl and cover with half a ladle of broth.

Serve, accompanied by Four Cents (see p. 100), Lu'sknikn (see p. 99), or Pipnaqn (see p. 110).

Serves 4–6
Preparation time:
1 hour, 15 minutes

- -

3 partridge breasts
4 medium potatoes,
　quartered
1 turnip, diced
3 carrots, sliced
water
1 tsp (5 ml) salt
1/2 tsp (2 ml) pepper

In the age of social media, news of people's passing, the birth of children, or any other notable event gets shared in mass-produced form through Facebook and other platforms. Long before social media, the way the church bells tolled indicated that a resident had died; a resident would run from one end of the reserve to the other to carry the news, sharing it in Mi'kmaq as he ran.

Chow Chow

Gordon Francis

Dinner was the best meal of the day, and, no matter our age, we'd have tea with our dinner. I'd add just enough milk 'til it got to be the perfect colour, then I knew it was going to be a great meal because tea goes so well with our food.

–Gordon Francis

Like corn, tomatoes originate from what is now Latin America, quickly becoming part of the European diet early in the colonial period. This highlights how Indigenous foodstuffs from the Americas have significantly impacted European and global cuisine—imagine Italian food without the humble tomato! Their presence in Mi'kmaq foodways is due to their introduction by settlers, who brought tomato seeds from Europe and began planting them in North America.

And like corn, the climate in New Brunswick is not the best for cultivating tomatoes due to the short growing season. By preserving them as in the following recipe, we can enjoy home-grown tomatoes all year. Canada's hothouse tomato industry comprises a significant agricultural export and thousands of migrant labourers

*Fish Cakes (see p. 11)
with Chow Chow.*

come to work in the country's greenhouses each year, many from the region from which tomatoes originate.

Chow chow is a fun way of using green tomatoes late in the harvest season when the fruit is turning red more slowly because of cooler temperatures. They are often picked just before the first frost of the season. (This is also a great way to use up tomatoes when your crop has grown beyond expectations!) The condiment draws together the poignancy of vinegar and the sweetness of sugar. The salt helps showcase the flavour of its star ingredient. This chow chow has a regular presence at the Sikniktuk dinner table and is commonly eaten alongside roasted or fried fish, pork chops, potatoes, and Lu'sknikn or Four Cents.

Chow chow is also known as green tomato relish and tomato chow. Some versions use red rather than green tomatoes, which draws in the sweetness of the ripened fruit. In the southern United States, it includes other pickled vegetables such as carrots, cauliflower, peppers, and cabbage. Its popularity there has been credited to the culinary influence of Acadians who fled from the Maritimes to Louisiana after the mid-eighteenth-century expulsion.

This recipe doesn't provide a specific amount of vinegar in the ingredients list as it depends on the size of your pot and how "vinegary" you like your condiments. The USDA recommends 4 cups (1 quart) vinegar for 10 pounds of tomatoes.

Yields 18 jars
Preparation time:
2 hours, plus time for
salting and bottling

----

10 lb (4.5 kg) green
    tomatoes, thinly
    sliced
6 onions, thinly sliced
1/2 cup (125 ml)
    pickling salt
pickling vinegar (as
    described on p. 61)
1 1/2 tsp (7 ml)
    pickling spice in a
    spice bag
3 cups (750 ml) sugar

Chow Chow RECIPE

Place tomatoes, onion, and salt in a large bowl. Toss so that everything is mixed evenly and the salt has coated everything.

Cover with a cloth and weigh down with a smaller bowl or frying pan. Place the bowl in the fridge and leave overnight. In the morning, drain all liquid from the bowl.

Place mixture in a large pot, add 2–3 inches (5–7.5 cm) vinegar before adding pickling spice and sugar. Add more sugar, to taste, but be careful not to add too much vinegar. Vinegar level should be about half the depth of the mixture.

Cover the pot, bring to a boil, and then lower heat, stirring often. Simmer for 2 hours or until tomatoes and onions are cooked.

Remove from the heat and let cool, and extract the bag of pickling spice.

Sanitize 18 mason jars using hot water; be sure to use new seals. Fill each bottle, leaving about 1 inch (2.5 cm) between the mixture and the top of the mason jar.

Bring a large pot filled with water to a rolling boil and boil jars for 10 minutes. Then carefully remove each bottle to a heat-safe surface and allow them to cool until the seals pop down. You can ensure this has happened because the lid will have a depression and should resist any attempt to push the lid down. If the seals don't pop within 24 hours, refrigerate the affected jars and use within 2 weeks. Properly sealed jars of Chow Chow can be kept in a cool, dark place for months.

The origin of the name "chow" is disputed. Some historians believe it was borrowed from the French word "chou" (cabbage), which is often pickled using the same process outlined in Gordon Francis's recipe, whereas others believe it is an English descriptive term for mixed vegetables from China and India that entered into common usage in the nineteenth century. A similar term in Spanish, "chaufa," refers to a stir-fry in Peru. When rendered as chow chow, rather than chow, it explicitly refers to pickled condiments, whether cucumbers or other vegetables, popular in North America.

Food Storage

Before refrigerators and freezers became common—and even before the introduction of electricity in Mi'kmaq communities in the mid-twentieth century—there were other means of storing food.

One method still used today across Sikniktuk is canning. Canning requires a large pot with a cover, clean mason jars, and new lids each time. Whether lobster, moose, jams made from wild fruit, or condiments made from vegetables, the water is brought to a boil and the full, sealed jars are immersed in water for ten to fifteen minutes, then removed to cool. You'll hear that lovely pop from the lids, indicating the process has worked.

Salting is used for preserving meat and fish, which are then stored in either a container with the salt, suspended in a dry spot and eaten as one would consume jerky, or rehydrated after adding to soups. Today, most people buy salt pork, rather than make their own. One encounters moose jerky from time to time—different from pemmican, which is made of berries and ground-up fatty meat. Jerky involves salting and drying meat, which toughens its texture. Its high salt content makes it a restorative snack, as it can be eaten raw or used as a seasoning in stew. The term jerky—and its preservation method—comes from Indigenous Meso-America, meaning ch'arki in Quechua. In Sikniktuk, moose jerky exemplifies the trans-Indigenous nature of foodways embraced in the region, with an Incan preservation process and term commingling with a traditional Mi'kmaw food source.

Many fresh vegetables—particularly tubers including potatoes, turnips, cabbages, carrots, parsnips, and onions—can be stored in a pantry that offers an ideal environment for the longer-term storage of foods that are not treated with salt or vinegar to last until the following harvest. (Most vegetables do not need the cold temperatures of a fridge.) Anne Barlow advises storing vegetables—particularly potatoes—so they're not touching each other. It's also important that they are dry before going into storage; these two steps will ensure that they will last a long time.

Historically, the pantry often served as an intermediate storage solution until the ground was frozen enough to provide cold storage. Many

Various preserves, including chow chow, beets, apple sauce, and maple syrup.

Mi'kmaq who did not have a dirt floor basement recall their pantry being a dug-out somewhere in the ground of their house where it remained cool year-round. And families had dug-out spaces outside, often lined with ice and seaweed that they brought from the river, or sometimes with wood, where berries and meat, as well as butter and cream, could be stored well into the spring.

Rabbits and fowl, gutted but not skinned, were strewn up along a covered porch in the winter months where they would stay cool, and even freeze, until the family was ready to consume them.

Most families also used their wells to store milk and butter. Where several households shared a well, it was common to find baskets suspended on ropes down the length of the well where the temperature was cool year-round. During the warmer months, a cover—a round piece of wood or a shed-like structure—help keep the well cool.

As readers learned in *The Story of Falling into the Well* (see p. 3), children were typically tasked with bringing water from the well to the house, which usually involved a little pail that even the littlest ones could carry. But—and Linda Sock remembers this well—their lack of balance meant that so much water sloshed out of the buckets that several trips were required! Even when water pipes were introduced in Lennox Island and other communities, their presence didn't necessarily translate into running water in each home. Marlene Thomas grew up mostly with running water, but it had to be fetched from the hydrant, shared by three or four families.

The flavour and texture of some foods can change according to how they're stored. Cranberries are a good example. Early in the fall, they are oval in shape and green in colour. Gertrude Nicholas and her uncle Archie Barlow lived near an important source of cranberries in Indian Island. He would bring Gertrude a bag of white, green, and red cranberries, which she then sorted by colour into separate brown paper bags. If she wanted to ripen the white or green ones, she would lay them in the warm autumn sun, turning them occasionally, until they turned red. Green cranberries can also be transformed into a canned jelly popular at the Christmas table, so that both red and green cranberry jellies accompany the meal.

The form and texture of blueberries also varied depending on how they were preserved. Interestingly, blueberries were cooked into a paste, dried on a white sheet on a hot summer day, and sewn into a pouch that was later hung on a string inside the house. Elizabeth Levi remembers her grandmother reconstituting the dried blueberry mix with water and eating it with Lu'sknikn in the winter months.

Winter

The Story of the Four Rabbits

Gordon Francis remembers learning, as a child, how to hunt deer and moose from the men in his family. His grandfather, uncles, and father would go out as a pack and set up camp in the woods. They always came home with rabbits, and now and again a moose, which they would share with the community. At the age of ten, it was Gordon's turn to start contributing to his family's dinner table by snaring rabbits.

One sunny winter afternoon after Gordon had returned home from setting his snares, he found himself doubled over in agony. He thought he was dying, so naturally he turned to a higher authority to negotiate what should happen next, praying, "Father—oh! Don't let me die. I have six snares in the woods right now. Just give me four rabbits tomorrow, make this pain go away, and maybe let me live 'til I'm forty?" Gordon didn't know it yet, but the excess gas trapped in his digestive tract led to the pain and caused him to reach out to God with his profound concern that if he died, any rabbits he trapped would go to waste.

After he finished his prayer that night, Gordon eventually managed to fall asleep. His job was to head out at around 5 A.M. to check his snares, then come home and get the stove going. He felt better when he awoke the next day and went into the woods.

Gordon approached his first snare and was pleased to see a rabbit, which he removed and put in his bag. Sure enough, a second rabbit awaited him in the second snare, which he removed and put in his bag, and another in the third snare, which he deposited in his bag. Excited that his prayers had been answered, given that his abdomen no longer hurt and he already had collected three rabbits, he turned to the fourth snare, which had only some remnants of a rabbit, because an owl had come and feasted on it. He shook out the leavings for another animal to finish.

The fifth trap offered no rabbit, but as fortune would have it, a fourth rabbit awaited Gordon in the last of his snares. So, he had his four rabbits, just as he had bargained.

The years passed and Gordon, with an excellent memory, remembers the year he turned forty. He recalled the deal he made with God. It so frightened him, he started going to the doctor for any stomach ache, bump, and rash, for fear that these symptoms might foretell the end.

After a few months, his doctor—recognizing the sudden increase in Gordon's preoccupation with his health—asked him, "You're here almost every day. What's going on? Are you a hypochondriac?" Gordon told him the story of the four rabbits and his deal with God to sort out his gas pains so that he could empty his snares and make sure his rabbits didn't go to waste. His doctor dryly replied: "Sounds explosive! But I don't think God would do that to you."

Molasses Cake

Lucy R. Milliea

Lucy and her cousin Joan were born and raised in their grandmother's house in Big Cove, along with thirteen cousins and siblings, and six aunts and uncles. Lucy's mother had died when she was only two, so her grandmother played a significant role in her life. With twenty-two mouths to feed, we imagine the following recipe was tripled or even quadrupled to ensure everyone could enjoy some cake!

Each year we planted extra potatoes, which we'd put aside and use to seed the next year's harvest. –Lucy R. Milliea

Molasses was imported to Atlantic Canada by Europeans during the transatlantic sugar and rum trade that flourished after their invasion of the Americas. Molasses is made by reducing sugarcane, or even beets, until a thick consistency and toasted colour emerge.

But when the Mi'kmaq first encountered molasses, they would have found it to be similar to tree syrup they had been making from maple and birch trees. Today maple syrup, which can only be produced in cold climates and is one of Maritime Canada's most well-known exports, far outpaces molasses in popularity. We can say that maple syrup is an Indigenous ingredient that has now infiltrated the cuisines of many cultures around the world!

Molasses was a common ingredient given to Mi'kmaq families by the Indian Agent. Its rich sweetness and sticky texture was a welcome flavourful addition. Molasses can be used as a spread for breads, sometimes with butter. Some children in Lucy's household didn't care for potatoes, so for Sunday

In late winter, sap is collected from trees using buckets such as these ones, after which it is reduced in a large pot or vat to produce maple syrup.

Lucy R. Milliea and Joan Clement's grandmother, Isabelle Augustine, was a **medicine woman**. She would grind up or shred dried acorns (mimgwaqn) that grow in the area as an antidote for diarrhea.

dinner their grandmother would make a side of Four Cents (see p. 100) smothered in molasses. And Gordon Francis prefers to dunk his fish cakes (see p. 10) in molasses, which he enjoys with a cup of steaming tea. Baked beans in Elsipogtog and Indian Island, called Ghost Beans, excluded molasses because molasses was used to flavour so many other dishes. By using salt pork, the available seasonings could be spread out and enjoyed in as many dishes as possible.

Today, health-related considerations have impacted how molasses and other sugars are used. Marlene Thomas excludes molasses from her baked bean recipe because people in her household have diabetes. But she also makes sure to include dried mustard powder as an antidote to the flatulence often experienced after consuming baked beans. In this recipe, the molasses brings a slight sweetness to the cake. Should you desire it sweeter, add a cup of white sugar.

Elder Joan Clement.

Lucy and Joan's recipe for fry bread tastes great topped with butter and molasses.

Combine 2 cups (500 ml) flour, 2 tsp (10 ml) baking powder, 1 tbsp (15 ml) sugar, and 1/2 tsp (2 ml) salt. Add 1 cup (250 ml) water and mix until dough forms.

Divide and form into 12 balls while warming a frying pan with canola oil.

Flatten each one into 1-inch- (2.5-cm-) thick patties and fry until brown on both sides. Serve warm.

Molasses Cake RECIPE

Preheat the oven to 350°F (175°C).

In a stand-mixer bowl fitted with the paddle attachment, mix flour, molasses, salt, ginger, eggs, and shortening. A wooden spoon and a large bowl can also be used.

In a separate large bowl, add baking soda to hot tea. It will fizz, so be sure the bowl is large enough to contain the reaction. Pour this mixture into the stand-mixer bowl and fold well until a consistent batter forms.

Transfer to a 13- x 9-inch (33- x 23-cm) greased baking pan. Bake for 40 minutes or until a toothpick inserted in the middle comes out clean.

Let cool for 10 minutes in the pan before cutting into squares and removing to a plate to serve. When ready to enjoy, spread butter on a warm piece and sip a cup of strong black tea.

Serves 8–12 squares
Preparation time:
60 minutes

- -

4 cups (1 L) flour
1 cup (250 ml) molasses
1 tsp (5 ml) salt
1/2 tsp (2 ml) ginger (optional)
3 eggs
1/2 cup (125 ml) shortening (or lard, oil, butter, or margarine), at room temperature, plus more for greasing cake pan
1 tsp (5 ml) baking soda
1 1/2 cups (375 ml) hot black tea

Boiled Dinner with Neck Bones

Eunice Augustine

Growing up in a family with six siblings, Eunice Augustine remembers rearing pigs and chickens and, like many people in the community, salting fresh pork to preserve it for months at a time. When a pig was ready to be butchered just before winter, her dad took it into town and returned with an abundance of meat. He always left the pig's head with the butcher, who made headcheese, half of which was returned to Eunice's home to be eaten with crackers or toast.

Marlene Thomas calls this preparation potted meat. In her family, the meat from the head was preserved as a spread or pâté that they enjoyed on sandwiches. Sometimes, though, her father would boil the pig's head until it was tender and white; he then placed it on a platter at the table where Marlene and her siblings delighted in what they thought was the most superb part of the pig.

As well as pig head, which includes the irresistible cheeks, brain, and skin (which when fried and salted makes for an amazing crackling), another offcut comes from the pig's back. Known as neck bones, the spine is one of the most succulent, if overlooked, parts of the pig. While the bones have less meat compared to ribs (although they are a fine substitute), the fat and flavour that the marrow imparts make them a significant addition to sauces and soups. The salting process further intensifies the meat's flavour. Neck bones are also a nutritious source of calcium, iron, protein, and vitamin B12.

We used to fertilize the garden using crushed eggshells and seaweed, which we'd get from the shore and let dry for a bit. Then, we'd break it up into smaller pieces, mix with the shells, and distribute into the soil before planting.

–Eunice Augustine

Eunice learned this recipe by watching her mother—a common way for food knowledge to get passed down through generations. Sometimes she makes homemade bread to sop up the juices.

While this boiled dinner calls for salted segments of spine, fresh pork can be used with bones such as shanks with marrow to flavour the broth.

Boiled Dinner with Neck Bones RECIPE

Serves 4
Preparation time:
3 hours, plus time to
soak the pork

2.2 lb (1 kg) salt pork
   neck bones
1 turnip, quartered
4 large carrots,
   chopped into 1-inch
   (2.5-cm) segments
4 potatoes, halved
1 green cabbage, cored
   and cut in wedges

Drain neck bones from brine and rinse in cold water. Return them to their container and cover with fresh water; refrigerate overnight. Drain brine again and rinse in fresh water.

Place neck bones in a deep pot and cover with cold water. Bring to a boil, reduce to medium, and continue to boil for 2 hours, covered, checking occasionally on the water level to ensure the meat does not dry out.

Taste the stock to assess seasoning. To reduce saltiness, remove a quarter of the liquid and replace with fresh water. The removed stock will be full of flavour; freeze to use another day to make Lu'sknikn (see p. 99), or in a soup or rice recipe.

Add turnip to the pot and boil for 30 minutes. Add carrots and potatoes, cook 5 minutes, and add cabbage. Boil for a further 15 minutes or until potatoes are tender. Ladle ingredients into bowls, cover with broth, and serve with Four Cents (see p. 100) or Lu'sknikn.

(Left) Freshly caught smelts from the Richibucto River are dusted with seasoned flour and pan-fried in butter.

(Right) Jasmine Pauze and Margaret Augustine clean the smelts before cooking them.

Smelts (gaqpesaq) are a popular late-winter fish throughout the Maritimes. This small, oily variety of fish spawns in rivers when they are still mostly covered with ice. Traditionally, the Mi'kmaq caught them by creating a weir or trap using whatever material was on hand—ice, rocks, and wood—that acted as a cage. They extended the device across the pathway of spawning fish, which swam into the weir and found themselves trapped in a net or basket positioned just upstream.

Today, ice fishing is enjoyed along the shores of the Richibucto and other rivers, with fishers cutting holes in the water and using poles to catch fish. Smelts are best when coated with seasoned flour and fried in butter until both sides are brown; top with a squeeze of lemon and eat right away with French fries.

Wiusey Petaqn (Meat Pie with Pork)

Shirley Milliea

Shirley Milliea's father wove chairs using flexible varieties of wood (particularly dogwood, called tupsi), and went into Rexton and the surrounding community with his horse Maude to sell them. With his earnings, he procured special foods like pork that his family did not produce or receive in rations.

When Shirley was a little girl, one day her father brought home a small pig, and she and her sister Ida Augustine were tasked with taking care of their new friend and preparing special meals from leftover vegetables and peelings. As the months passed, the pig grew and grew, until one cold day when Shirley was away, the pig was slaughtered. Shirley admits that, despite missing her friend, the pig she had so carefully raised tasted delicious.

Meat pies have been part of the Mi'kmaq diet for centuries. It's a flexible dish that can include whatever is in season or in excess in the pantry. Georgina Barlow, who grew up in Eel Ground, remembers eating what she calls Miramichi Meat Pie with salt pork, sometimes fresh pork, onions, and both apples and raisins, making it a sweet and savoury dish. Other versions substitute beef and moose meat for pork. Everybody remembers eating meat pie at Easter and other special days. A key distinguishing aspect is that, unlike most meat pies today, it is sealed with a layer of meat-infused dough.

This meat pie with pork, Petaqn, is eaten at Christmas, so it is easy to double or triple the recipe to accommodate a crowd. While it can be prepared in a round pie dish, Shirley prefers a rectangular pan. Placed next to the turkey on Christmas Day, Petaqn is considered a delicacy. Shirley learned this recipe from her mother, who sometimes layered potatoes rather than Lu'sknikn to crown the pie. While her mother made it in their wood oven, she would fry potato slices on the stove top to make chips for

My dad always fished salmon and he'd watch my mum salt it for the winter months. And now I cook the potatoes but my husband peels them for me, which is nice because peeling can sometimes discolour your hands, and you wouldn't want to do that—I have such nice hands!
—Shirley Milliea

Shirley and her siblings, who eagerly observed the process until their treat was ready

This recipe involves two processes—first is the preparation of the meat, and then the Lu'sknikn, which for this recipe is made differently than the standard recipe on page 99.

Wiusey Petaqn RECIPE

For filling, place salt pork in a large pot and add enough water to cover. Place on high heat, cover when it starts boiling, and reduce to medium. Boil for at least 2 hours until tender, checking water level occasionally to ensure the mixture does not dry out. If the water tastes too salty, change liquid and boil meat in fresh water for another hour.

When tender, allow meat to cool in its cooking juices. Remove pork from the pot, remove bones, and cut it and fresh pork into small cubes (do not dispose of fat as it will help keep the dish moist later). Reserve 1 cup (250 ml) pork juices for Lu'sknikn recipe, skimming any fat.

Place cubed meat in a stainless-steel bowl with onions, and season with pepper. Cover the bowl with plastic wrap and refrigerate overnight.

For Lu'sknikn crust, preheat oven to 400°F (204°C).

Mix flour and baking powder in a bowl, and cut in lard. Work it in the mixture by hand until it has a coarse consistency. Make a well in the middle and slowly add pork juice. Gently blend into flour mixture by hand, adding more water, if necessary. Do not overmix the dough. Let rest for a few minutes before using.

Grease 2 (8-inch/20-cm) square pans. Cut dough into four parts and, using a rolling pin, roll two slightly larger than the pan and about 1/2 inch (1.3 cm) thick. Line the pans with the rolled-out dough so that the dough extends 1 inch (2.5 cm) beyond the pan.

Equally divide the refrigerated meat and onion mixture between the two pans.

Roll two more pieces of dough the same thickness as before and place over the meat mixtures.

cont'd on 80

Yields 2 pies
Preparation time:
2 hours, 30 minutes to prepare the meat; 60 minutes to assemble.

- - - - - - - - - - - - - - - - - -

For filling
2.2 lb (1 kg) salt pork
2.2 lb (1 kg) fresh pork, preferably roast or another cut on the bone
2 large onions, finely diced
2 tsp (10 ml) black pepper, or to taste

For Lu'sknikn
4 cups (1 L) all-purpose flour
8 tsp (40 ml) baking powder
1 cup (250 ml) lard
1 cup (250 ml) pork juice (reserved from boiling pork)
1 egg (optional)
1 tbsp (15 ml) water (optional)

Trim excess dough and then use your fingers to pinch together the bottom and top dough layers, forming pleats around the perimeter.

Cut three slits into the top crusts to allow steam to escape during baking. For a golden-brown colour, whisk an egg with 1 tbsp (15 ml) water and brush it on the top crust using a pastry brush.

Bake for 20 minutes at 400°F (204°C), then decrease to 375°F (190°C) for another 20 minutes, until the crust browns.

Barley Soup

Janice Augustine

Whether for a baby shower, for the day children returned from residential school, or for a wake celebrating the life of a community member, this recipe has always been intended for special occasions. The history of its signature ingredient and the star of Janice Augustine's recipe—barley—amplifies its importance for eastern North American Indigenous

Marlene Thomas always reaches for beef barley soup. It brings her comfort, reminds her of the security of being home, and the importance of family: "My favourite soup growing up was beef barley soup. When I went away, like to residential school, my welcome-home meal was beef barley soup."

diets. Soups are an egalitarian dish that bubbles with the maker's generosity when given to the community or to guests invited into the home.

In Mi'kmaq communities, soup makes use of both seasonal and ingredients that are on hand. By frying and then simmering ingredients, the depth of flavour transforms the soup's stock from plain water into a seasoned and complex dish. Fat adds body, whereas aromatics and salted meats season the soup. Barley increases the nutritional value of the meal and provides texture.

Back then, rabbit was so tasty; even the heart was wonderful, and I'd eat it all the time. Today it's harder to find and doesn't taste the same. –Janice Augustine

While most barley consumed in Canada originates from the Middle East or Africa, it was also planted in the Atlantic region by settler farmers. A variety of grain called little barley (*hordeum pusillum*) traditionally provided a significant source of nutrition. Once dried, it was ground or left in the form of meal, and then incorporated into breads and stews. Little barley grew throughout the Americas and was replaced with maize, and later flour and barley brought by Europeans. By the nineteenth century, Mi'kmaq farmers were planting barley alongside their other important potato and wheat crops.

Many of the contributors to this cookbook recall observing members of their family preparing a barley soup. Elizabeth Levi watched her grandmother make beef barley soup, and later in life when she went to prepare it herself, she marvelled at how her grandmother achieved such a flavoursome broth.

The rich colour of the soup's broth develops from coating the beef in flour and then browning it. Deglazing the pan afterward with liquid ensures that the caramelized bits sticking to the bottom of the pot influence both

Herman J. Simon recalls a traditional technique his father employed during winter to hunt deer and moose. He and a couple others would go into the forest on snowshoes with enough food to last two or three days. Once they began to see deer tracks, they'd dig a hole in the snow as deep as possible—four to five feet, if they could manage it—then they'd cover the hole with branches and brush, and wait. Deer, and moose if the hole was big enough, would fall into their trap. They'd use a knife to finish the job.

the flavour and look of the soup. Elizabeth asked her grandmother for her secret, to which she replied: "Just take a tea bag and throw it in there and then take it out!" We now know Mi'giju' Malian's secret for her fabulous beef barley soup.

Barley Soup RECIPE

Place flour on a plate and season with salt. Chop meat into cubes and coat evenly, shaking off any excess.

Heat oil in a medium-sized pot on the stove on high heat. Add onions and meat. After browning the meat on each side, slowly add water to the pot (avoid that hot steam!) and using a wooden spoon, scrape the browned bits from the bottom of the pan to flavour the soup.

Cover and simmer for about an hour, then add barley and simmer for another 25–30 minutes.

Add carrots and potatoes. If desired, add tomatoes. Cook for another 20–30 minutes.

The soup is ready when the potatoes are tender. Serve with Tea Biscuits (see p. 102), Pipnaqn (see p. 110), Lu'sknikn (see p. 99), or Four Cents (see p. 100).

Serves 4
Preparation time:
2 hours, 10 minutes

- - - - - - - - - - - - - - - - - -

1 tbsp (15 ml) all-purpose flour
salt, to taste
1 lb (450 g) beef or moose stew meat
1 onion, sliced
1 tbsp (15 ml) oil
4 cups (1 L) cold water
1/2 cup (125 ml) pearl barley
2 carrots, sliced
3 potatoes, cubed
1/4 cup (60 ml) diced fresh or canned tomatoes (optional)

In Mi'kmaq, beef comes from "French moose" (wenuj tia'm), a term that acknowledges the culture responsible for introducing cows to the region: wenuj, meaning "French," and "tia'm," moose. The two meats are often used interchangeably—don't be afraid to try Janice's recipe with moose meat!

Annie's Soup

Vincent Simon

Annie and Harry Peterpaul were the godparents of Vincent Simon—becoming something nearer to grandparents over time—helping to raise the future chief of Elsipogtog. They took Vincent and his nine siblings, and their immediate and extended families, to Maine each year for harvesting. That's where Vincent met his future wife, Sarah Simon, who was there with her eleven siblings, parents, and extended family for the harvest season.

Just as soon as we returned from blueberry picking season in Maine, which starts in July, the truck from Limestone would come and pick us up to go off potato picking in September.
–Vincent Simon

Sarah—also Annie's relation through marriage—recalls the one time she was tempted to experiment with Annie's soup recipe by frying the beef first. Frying ground beef allows it to brown and develop flavour; this is why we usually fry it before adding it to a sauce for spaghetti, for instance. At the same time, though, the fat content of the meat transforms, depending on the way it is cooked. When Sarah added the fried beef to the soup, the dish didn't taste the same because the fullness from the meat's fat that Annie boils off into a rich stock is an important component and gives this soup its "Annie flavour."

This soup is so beloved in Sikniktuk that it was christened Annie's Soup, even while Annie was still alive.

Annie's Soup RECIPE

Place beef, salt, and water in a deep pot, and mash the meat with a wooden spoon so that it covers the bottom of the pot. Leave on high heat until it starts boiling, breaking apart any remaining larger chunks. Once a rolling boil is achieved, reduce the heat to medium, add potatoes and tomatoes, and cook for 15 minutes.

Add rotini and cook for another 15 minutes on low heat until the pasta is tender. Add pepper.

Serve with Pipnaqn (see p. 110) or Four Cents (see p. 100).

Serves 4
Preparation time:
45 minutes

- - - - - - - - - - - - - - - - - - -

1 lb (450 g) ground
   beef
2 tsp (10 ml) salt
6 cups (1.4 L) water
3 large russet
   potatoes, diced
19-oz (540-g) can
   whole tomatoes,
   diced
1 cup (250 ml) rotini
pepper, to taste

Annie and Harry Peterpaul harvesting blueberries in Maine.

Rabbit Stew

Sarah Simon

Called wapus in Mi'kmaq, wild rabbits are best snared in the winter when their fur is white, which signals that the rabbit is still tender. Their whiteness also coincides with the winter snow, as rabbits survive better from natural predators with fur that blends in with the winter landscape. Rabbit snares are laid out at night and checked the next morning. Sarah Simon remembers how her grandfather hunted and fished seasonally; he would visit her mother each day with whatever the family needed or desired, making him something like their own supermarket. Sarah and her siblings had to clean whatever he brought—eel, salmon, and, of course, rabbit.

Because of climate change, rabbits are no longer easy to obtain in the community. With less snow, there are fewer rabbits. They are also pursued by other animals, whose food sources have also been reduced over the years. The habitat for rabbits and other game has changed by what we call "progress" or "development" by settlers who build subdivisions, businesses, golf courses, etc., on land that otherwise would have been used for hunting, trapping, and snaring. This encroachment and restricted access to hunting, despite Mi'kmaq treaty rights, has impacted the intergenerational knowledge of snaring rabbit and the taste for this traditional protein source.

Uncle Herman Simon remembers making rabbit stew somewhat differently than the method outlined on page 88. After snaring and skinning the rabbit, he slices along its belly to remove the innards. He always leaves intact the liver and heart, and tries to conserve as much of the blood as possible for flavouring the stew. He places the rabbit, innards removed but otherwise

Raking blueberries in Maine was like living on a small reserve. There are lots of folks from back home and also from so many other parts of the Maritimes—you see them constantly for two to three weeks at a time. There were so many of us hailing from different communities, whereas at home we tend to see the same people day in and day out, making raking a really special time of the year.
–Sarah Simon

Rabbit was Elizabeth Levi's favourite food growing up. Her grandmother would snare rabbits and prepare them stuffed with sliced potatoes, and fresh cranberries when they were in season in late summer.

whole, in a pot of water, being careful not to let the blood spill out-side the pot. He then adds onions and any seasoning. (Herman's mother used finely chopped salt pork.) He cooks the rabbit for several hours on low heat, and in the last half hour or so adds cubed potatoes, carrots, or turnips—whatever is on hand—and cooks until tender, allowing the broth to thicken like a gravy.

Many people are no longer accustomed to eating rabbit. Sarah recalls when her youngest son, at about eight, walked into her mother's house and smelled the aroma of what promised to be a mouth-watering meal. He had never had rabbit, and Sarah was afraid he would refuse because he was unfamiliar with it. His wise mother knew he would like it if he didn't know what it was first, so she told him it was chicken stew. Her suspicions were confirmed when he devoured two bowls. It was a hit! Now he loves it every time!

Rabbit Stew RECIPE

Serves 4
Preparation time:
4 hours, 30 minutes

- -

1 rabbit, if store-
    bought; or 2–3
    rabbits, if snared
2 onions, diced
2 tsp (10 ml) salt
3–4 cups (750 ml–1L)
    rabbit blood, or
    low-sodium pork or
    beef stock
2 large potatoes,
    quartered
2 turnips, quartered
    (optional)
2 carrots, quartered
    (optional)
pepper, to taste

Clean rabbit and cut into 6 pieces, discarding the head. Ask your butcher or hunter to reserve blood for the stew.

Place rabbit in a large pot and fill with water; add onions, salt, and blood or stock, and cover.

Bring the pot to a boil and then reduce to low, simmering for about 4 hours until the meat is tender.

Add potatoes and cook for another 15 minutes. If desired, add turnip and carrots. Season with pepper.

Once vegetables are tender, the stew is ready to serve. Ladle rabbit, vegetables, and some flavoursome cooking liquid into a bowl for each diner. Accompany with Four Cents (see p. 100).

Mary Jane Simon (Levy) and John Simon, Herman J. and Freda May's parents, pictured in this undated photo, likely from the 1920s.

Fats

Many of the recipes in this book suggest fat alternatives because the colonial history of cooking fats has made an indelible impression upon Mi'kmaq foodways. Traditionally, foods were prepared in boiling water over a fire, whereas today we fry more food and incorporate additional fat into dishes. The fat sources—cows for butter, and pigs for salt pork and lard—are not native species in Sikniktuk. Their incorporation into the Mi'kmaw diet emphasizes the way colonial food practices have become blended with traditional ones.

For example, owning cows wasn't the most common practice in Sikniktuk, as Mi'kmaq traditionally did not keep and raise animals in the way that settlers do today. Elizabeth Levi recalls that her Mi'giju' had a cow and would collect milk each day to share with her extended family. She also made butter and cream and distributed it. The presence of cows, of course, implies the presence of infrastructure to support them—from barns, to troughs, to fences—which many families found challenging because raising animals to eat or for milk and butter is not part of traditional Mi'kmaq foodways. The Indian Agent also did not provide any support for raising animals. When the government gave each family a pig, for example, that pig was not accompanied by feed and the infrastructure needed to maintain it.

Decades ago, butter was not prioritized alongside flour, molasses, and sugar in a family's monthly rations. Butter—and substitutes like lard and margarine—either had to be purchased, obtained through trade, rendered from a cut of meat, or procured directly from livestock. When butter wasn't available, rendered fat became and continues to be a common substitute for cooking oil. The reserved drippings from bacon and salt pork re-solidify and can be used a spoonful at a time to fry and flavour pretty much anything. Families usually had a receptacle or container where rendered fat was deposited so that it could be used whenever it was desired—when frying Lu'sknikn or Four Cents, for example.

Lee Ann Sock recalls how her mother used to reserve bacon grease to incorporate into her bread recipe or for frying meat, which meant that she grew up without oil and butter as common staples in the kitchen. Later in life, though, her mother became more conscious of heart disease and other health conditions and traded in her bacon grease for shortening, and later for canola oil. Salt pork is another source of fat used in many of this book's recipes, particularly once the meat is rendered in a frying pan, stew, or casserole. Many older folks today, however, avoid salt pork and bacon due to high blood pressure.

Ironically, this awareness of health issues pushed people toward industry-created solutions for foods perceived to be poor for one's diet. Margarine was created in France in the mid-1800s as an economical butter substitute for the military and the poor. In the 1940s it was marketed as a healthy substitute for butter, as it has unsaturated fats rather than saturated fats that associated butter with heart disease. Many people remember it resembling lard because margarine in its original form is white. To make margarine look more like butter, yellow colouring had to be stirred in—a task left to children in Elsipogtog, and beyond, where colouring packets and margarine came home from the Indian Agent's store along with the family's rations. In more recent years margarine has been criticized (outside the US) for having trans fats, which increases cholesterol and causes heart disease, and for having the similar number of calories and amount of fat as butter.

Cheese is another dairy product for which there is no Indigenous history. Cheese was considered a luxury ingredient in Elsipogtog and the region, and it could not be sourced locally except from modern supermarkets. Even then, one had to buy an entire wheel, which would be something

The **fur trade** is often imagined as being more northern- and central-Canadian than firmly extending into the Maritime provinces. Herman and his sister, Freda May Augustine, however, remember how their father and uncle would trap rabbit and mink when they were growing up in Elsipogtog. The family always ate the meat, of course, but they didn't have much use for the remaining pelts, so their father sold them to the Hudson's Bay Company.

The company agent would keep a register of all the pelts and, just before Christmas, he'd issue a cheque to their father. This helped the Simon family enjoy a bountiful festive season—everybody got brand-new shoes, and sometimes the children could keep some fur to make rabbit-lined gloves for their mother as a Christmas gift. Using their fur trade earnings, their mother would also procure large amounts of wool, from which she knitted warm and water-absorbent wool socks for the children— just in time for the coldest months of the winter season.

of an investment. Gordon Francis remembers his parents taking a boat to the grocery store in Richibucto—it was quite an occasion because they would return with special items that they rarely ate. Gordon and his siblings would wait by the window, and on a clear night when the moon was full, they could see who approached by boat. When they finally spotted their parents, they'd run out and help them bring in the groceries. One of the first rewards from that shopping trip was a slice of cheese. His mother made sure everybody had a small slice. It was so fresh and soft, whereas any other kind of cheese Gordon had was hard and dried up because there was nowhere to store it properly.

Year-
Round

Traditional Indigenous Ingredients and Cooking Methods

Mi'kmaq Foods

Traditional Mi'kmaw food storage practices mean that most everything is available throughout the year in one form or another.

Berries
Blackberries, blueberries, chokecherries, cranberries, currants, elderberries, raspberries, and wild strawberries together comprise a significant source of vitamins and are harvested in mid-summer to late fall. These berries have grown in Mi'kma'ki for as long as anybody remembers and are nutritious for both humans and the non-human world. Importantly, they are foraged rather than cultivated. Berries are best eaten when picked fresh; when preserved, priority should be given to freezing them directly after harvesting to keep their nutrients. They can also be canned, preserved as a jam after being stewed, or dried and then rehydrated later in the season.

Nuts
Acorns, beechnuts, chestnuts, and groundnuts are harvested in the fall and can be eaten as a raw ingredient whole, roasted, or ground into a flour and then consumed year-round. Across the Americas, acorns, for example, are dried and ground into meal or flour from which a flat bread or a porridge can be made.

Grasses and Ferns
Sea sage, seaweed, and fiddleheads are readily available throughout the Maritimes. Fiddleheads, foraged in the spring, might be one of the only foodstuffs that settlers would consider a vegetable—boiled, or steamed inside a fish—within the traditional Mi'kmaw culinary world, which tends to be more protein and fruit heavy. Sea grasses are available year-round and used for flavouring and protecting food as it cooks.

Meats
Bear, caribou (before they disappeared from the region), deer, moose, porcupine, rabbit, seagulls, and small animals such as squirrels, comprise the land-based protein sources of the Mi'kmaq. Most are hunted in the fall or

winter when conditions are ideal—for instance, while the bear is sleepy from hibernating, and when the snow is white and the rabbit is young. Meats are typically consumed in a stew or soup after boiling or simmering them on a fire. Meats can also be dried or salted for storage and then used in soups later in the year.

Fish

Bass, clams, cod, eel, herring, lobster, oysters or quahogs, salmon, smelts, and trout are common aquatic protein sources. Cooking them in water with their shells and bones intact flavours the water while releasing fat, giving the broth more texture. Seafood can be eaten fresh or preserved through salting and drying. There is little reason to preserve seafood because it is plentiful year-round, except for bass which is available throughout the summer and fall. Today, it has become more common to fry fish, especially smelts.

Cleaning a smelt.

Trans-Indigenous Foods

Several significant vegetables that today influence Mi'kmaq foodways originate from other areas of the Indigenous world.

Oysters at a Lennox Island summer powwow.

Potatoes

This tuber hails from Meso-America and, after the invasion, Europeans added them to their diets, which is how they subsequently came to Mi'kma'ki—or so many presume through what is known as the Columbian Exchange (food crops, diseases, etc., between the new and old worlds). But oral traditions among various Indigenous groups, from the Haida to the Haudenosaunee, describe cultivating potatoes before European influence—through their complex, intercontinental communication and trade networks. Potatoes remain a staple in the Peruvian diet, and traditionally Incan people prepared them just as we do today—boiled, mashed, and roasted. Potatoes were cultivated in North America for the first time by settlers in the early 1700s; the crop flourishes in Mi'kma'ki.

Corn

First cultivated by Indigenous Peoples in southern Mexico and Peru, corn was a staple—eaten fresh, but more commonly dried and ground into a meal or paste to make tortillas and flatbreads. Corn is one of the "Three Sisters" grown as interdependent crops along with beans and squash. Europeans also added corn to their diets, resulting in its domestication in Europe. Today corn is a significant industry in North America, where it is used as a fuel source (ethanol), as a food thickener (cornstarch), as the foundation for popular beverages (bourbon), and for its nutritional value, fresh or frozen. Its presence in North America is not entirely due to Europeans, however, because trans-Indigenous trade networks ensured that corn was growing in North America centuries before Europeans invaded. The Haudenosaunee, for instance, have considered corn part of their diet since time immemorial, and it was cultivated in Maine as early as 1200 CE. They taught Europeans how to grow corn, and once imported back to Europe in early colonial times, it flourished during a period of food insecurity on that continent. Elders share that corn was grown in places such as Shediac before settlers came.

Tomatoes

From the Nahuatl word "tomatl" and originating from Indigenous Mexico, the tomato became an important part of the European diet because of how versatile and nutritious the fruit is. The Aztecs used tomatoes for sauces, including hot sauces, and to garnish dishes. Once Europeans returned home with the tomato in the early 1500s, it spread to other continents, turning up in China within decades. Tomatoes were first cultivated by settlers in the early 1700s and it wasn't until the last century that they began to be grown in Mi'kma'ki.

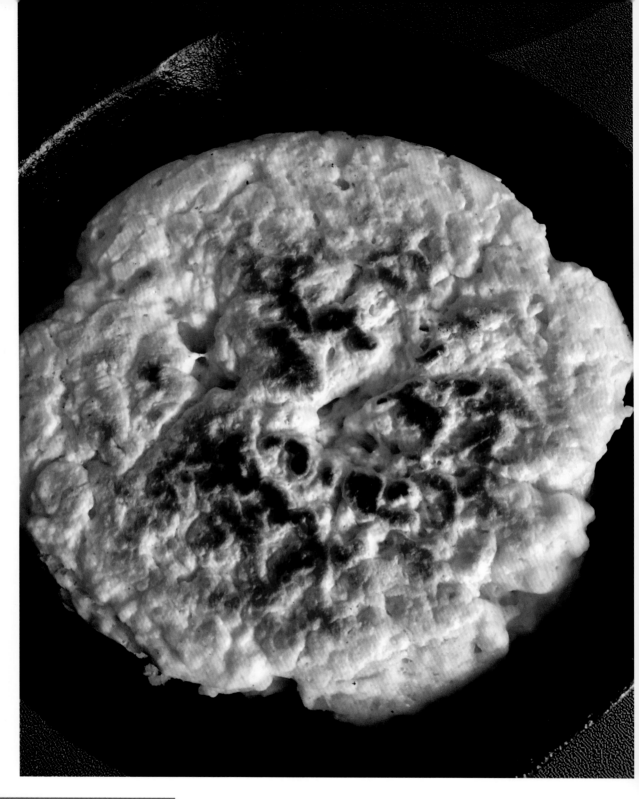

Lu'sknikn

L u'sknikn is the Mi'kmaw word for a flour-based crust that is considered by some as a form of Bannock. Lu'sknikn can accompany many meals and is also satisfying on its own as oven-fried bread.

Lu'sknikn RECIPE

Mix flour, baking powder, and salt in a bowl. Cut in lard. Work it in by hand until mixture is coarse.

Make a well in the middle and slowly add water. Gently blend into flour mixture with your hand, adding a bit more water if necessary. Do not overmix. Let rest for a few minutes.

When ready to bake, place dough in a greased 13- x 8-inch (33- x 20-cm) pan and bake at 350°F (175°C) for 35 minutes, until brown.

Lu'sknikn is perfect with stews, soups, and any other main course.

Serves 12
Preparation time:
45 minutes

----

4 cups (1 L) all-
    purpose flour
8 tsp (40 ml) baking
    powder
1 tsp (5 ml) salt
1 cup (250 ml) lard
1 cup (250 ml) water

Four Cents

Jake Sock

In the 1980s, now-retired RCMP officer Jake Sock and his wife, Geraldine, were vacationing in Florida when they happened upon billboards advertising an Indigenous dancing competition in Jacksonville. They joined the spectators who packed the stadium, where one of the food vendors caught Jake's attention. He watched the young man prepare a loose dough with flour and water before immersing it in the deep fryer. After a few moments it floated to the surface, signalling it was ready to be removed. The vendor cut through it lengthwise as if it was a hamburger bun, and then filled it with a buttery spread. Jake recognized that the man was making Four Cents, even though he was hundreds of miles away from home. It was certainly not the first time Jake had encountered the dish.

I can remember tasting my first egg salad sandwich with Coke on the way home from picking potatoes in Maine in the 1950s when I was about seven.
–Jake Sock

Jake's Mi'giju' Susie Ann taught him how to make Four Cents. He prepared it at his family's hunting camps in Midisaqamiktuk, a campsite near Elsipogtog First Nation and Salmon River Road. Each person had a job at camp, and Four Cents was Jake's contribution to sustaining the group. (His brother Howard Sock made the best duck stew when duck was in season.) "I can remember they used to love my Four Cents so much that they had me make it in the morning for breakfast," reflects Jake.

Four Cents gets its name from the four main (and cheap) ingredients, making this recipe one that anybody can prepare, regardless of their socio-economic situation. It is quick and truly versatile in that it can be eaten any time of day and complements any meal, whether eggs, oatmeal, beans, or stew. Dress it with butter and jam, or molasses, or leave it plain to dip in soups or sauces. A version of Four Cents called Sisla'gwa'taqn is popular. The batter for this fry bread is looser, like a pancake, which results in a thinner bread. A recommended variation is to use buckwheat rather than white flour. (Buckwheat pancakes are called poggwitewe'l.)

Jake's unique take on this dish is to sprinkle black pepper on it after the dough goes into a searing-hot cast-iron pan. He counsels us to always use ice water to prepare the dough, as it gives the bread its desired buoyancy and texture. Jake's parents would source ice from the river during the winter months and keep it in an ice box dug into the ground. But today, ice cubes from the freezer do the trick. This recipe suggests using one frying pan and repeating the frying process twice to yield two breads. If you have two frying pans, you can cook both fry breads simultaneously.

Four Cents RECIPE

Add 2 tbsp (30 ml) oil to a heavy bottom or cast-iron frying pan, place on low heat.

In a bowl, mix dry ingredients and then slowly add ice water, stirring with a whisk until the mixture forms a batter. The pan should now be warm enough to fry the dough.

Increase the heat to maximum and wait a couple moments to ensure it is hot—if the oil shimmers and you can slightly smell it, you can start frying bread. Pour half the batter into the pan and reduce the heat to low. Season with pepper. After 5 minutes, use a spatula to check if dough has formed a hard crust, and then turn it over. Pour remaining oil around the perimeter of the bread, shaking slightly to spread oil underneath it. Cook it for another 5 minutes or so, checking to ensure that it is brown but not burning.

Repeat these steps to cook remaining batter. Remove and serve with breakfast, lunch, dinner, or as a snack accompanied by butter and jam.

Yields 2 fry breads
Preparation time: 15 minutes

- - - - - - - - - - - - - - - - - -

3 tbsp (45 ml) oil
2 cups (500 ml) flour
3 tbsp (45 ml) baking powder
1/2 tsp (2 ml) salt
1 tsp (5 ml) sugar
1 cup (250 ml) ice water
black pepper, to taste

Tea Biscuits

Anita Joseph

Growing up with eighteen siblings and raised by her aunt and uncle in Elsipogtog, Anita watched and learned from Mi'giju' Susie Ann preparing food for the entire household. Mi'giju' would share knowledge, impart values, and remind the children how to be good members of their community. Each day, they would have at least one big meal featuring seasonal or preserved meat such as rabbit, deer, and moose, or fish such as bass, eel, and salmon, in addition to potatoes and a hearty soup.

Anita remembers learning to knead bread while standing on a chair beside her aunt. Mi'giju' often fed grieving families in the community, but even when there wasn't a loss, Mi'giju' prepared fifteen loaves of bread twice a week to share with the old man next door and her aunt across the road, as well as other neighbours.

This much cooking required resources that far exceeded what Anita's family would have received in rations. People in the community share what they have, so her Mi'giju' always had enough ingredients to prepare cookies, bread, and delicious and nutritious meals. Family members, whether uncles or cousins, would give her flour, maybe a couple chickens, a bucket of fish, and brown sugar. Neighbours would lend their soup bone so that she could prepare a flavoursome broth for soup, and then she'd pass that on to another neighbour.

The following recipe can be served with savoury or sweet dishes. Mi'giju' Susie Ann's favourite pairing was jam spread over a layer of salted butter.

I'll never forget my Mi'giju' growing up, how, when there was a death in the community, she'd start another pot of soup intended for the family. When I got older, she'd ask me to help her make cookies and tea biscuits to go with the soup. And at the same time, she'd get us to help her finish a blanket or quilt in time for the deceased's auction. She gave her efforts and labour to the community; she liked to nurture it during tough times.
–Anita Joseph

Sarah Annie Levi, Anita's great-niece, checking out the tea biscuits.

Anita Joseph's grandmother **Mi'giju' Susie Ann** was a beacon of love in the community. She recalls how dozens of children would swim in the Richibucto River behind her house, which was known as Mi'giju' Susie Ann's sitmug (beach). When they'd come up the hill after swimming all afternoon, the children were greeted by Mi'giju' Susie Ann's cookies—enough for everybody—usually chocolate chip (see p.115), peanut butter (see p. 118), or brown sugar drop cookies.

Yields 12 large tea biscuits
Preparation time: 45 minutes

- -

5 cups (1.1 L) all-purpose flour
1/4 cup (60 ml) baking powder
1 1/2–2 tsp (7–10 ml) salt
3/4 cup (175 ml) shortening
2 cups (500 ml) milk

Tea Biscuits RECIPE

Preheat the oven to 375°F (190°C).

In a large bowl, combine dry ingredients and cut in shortening, working it in until the mixture has the consistency of small peas.

Pour in milk gradually and stir until dough seems sticky. Using your fingers, knead briefly and shape into a ball.

Place the ball of dough on a floured surface, and roll dough until it is 1 inch (2.5 cm) thick. Use a cookie cutter or a round glass to create 12 circles in the dough and gently extract them.

Place parchment paper on a pan, or grease the pan and place tea biscuits so that they are almost touching. Bake for about 25–30 minutes until golden brown.

Some people like to use **buttermilk** in their tea biscuits for the tangy and creamy flavour it imparts. If you don't have buttermilk on hand, mix 1 tbsp (15 ml) vinegar or lemon juice for 1 cup (250 ml) milk. Let the mixture sit for a few minutes and then use as instructed in the recipe.

Anita Joseph removing a tray of biscuits from the oven at the Oetjgoapeniag Child and Family Centre in Elsipogtog.

Sisla'gwa'taqn (Fry Bread)

Joan Clement

L'nu tacos made with Fry Bread.

Flour might be considered one of the more colonizing elements of our shared foodways, because its integration into the western diet centuries ago came after Europeans developed a taste for particular varieties of ground grain, such as buckwheat. These grains became a bedrock for many Indigenous diets.

Buckwheat originated in Asia. Hundreds of years ago it spread along trade networks through Asia and Africa, and eventually infiltrated European food culture in the medieval period. It became part of the Mi'kmaw diet through interactions with Acadians who settled in Atlantic Canada in the seventeenth century. By the late eighteenth century, buckwheat was broadly cultivated in the region. When the Acadians brought buckwheat to the Americas, it was already a staple in the French diet where it was incorporated into breads, and eventually became the preferred flour for crepes stuffed with cheese, meats, vegetables, and even eggs (called *galettes* in France).

The Acadian version of fry bread, called *ployes,* is made with the same ingredients as Joan's fry bread, but rather than frying the patties on both sides, it is cooked only on one side so that bubbles form on the top, giving it a different texture.

Joan remembers her grandfather cultivating buckwheat. After harvesting it, he brought it to a mill in town so that it could be turned into flour. This flour has a nuttier and more profound flavour than regular white flour, so it makes for a great substitute in flat bread recipes. It is also a complex carbohydrate and a healthy addition to one's diet.

After my father went to Europe for the war, we lived with my grandparents. They always had a big garden, and we had animals and horses and cows and pigs and chickens. So, it was a big farm. And we never ate margarine! Only homemade butter. –Joan Clement

Sisla'gwa'taqn is thicker than Four Cents and has the consistency of a patty before being deep-fried, whereas Four Cents has a pancake-like batter that is poured into a hot frying pan,

The following recipe will make four meal-size L'nu tacos. Layer toppings onto the bread and either eat as you normally would a taco, or tackle it with a knife and fork.

Sisla'gwa'taqn (Fry Bread) RECIPE

Yields 4 breads
Preparation time:
20 minutes, plus time
for assembling tacos

- -

1 1/2 cups (375 ml)
    all-purpose flour (or
    replace one third
    with buckwheat
    flour)
2 tsp (10 ml) baking
    powder
1/2 tsp (2 ml) salt
1 tbsp (15 ml) sugar
1/2 cup (125 ml) water
2 cups (500 ml)
    cooking oil

Combine dry ingredients in a mixing bowl, then add water and mix well with a fork.

Turn dough onto a floured surface and knead until it reaches the consistency of bread dough, adding a touch more water or flour, if necessary.

Cut dough into 4 pieces. Working in batches, flatten 1 piece using your hands and stretch the dough until it is about 4 inches (10 cm) in diameter.

Heat oil in a pan on high heat until it starts to shimmer. Gently lower each stretched dough patty into the pan, working in batches.

Fry dough for about 2 minutes until it becomes golden. Turn with kitchen tongs and cook for another 2 minutes, then remove and serve warm.

L'nu tacos are a favourite at gatherings, including powwows (mawiomi'l). A version of them can be found in many Indigenous communities across North America. The Mi'kmaw variety uses the fry bread as one would a tortilla shell, as the vehicle for the taco's filling or toppings. Ladle onto it tomato sauce with fried ground beef, and top with shredded iceberg lettuce and cheese. Some people add salsa and sour cream as well. Enjoy!

Qonesuwey (Stew)
Anita Francis

Qonesuwey traditionally includes salt pork as its main protein, which today one might find in supermarkets throughout Sikniktuk in the preserved meat area alongside bacon and smoked sausage. Often coming from the belly region of the animal—although other cuts can be used as well—the meat is cured using salt. The process has existed for centuries. In the early 1900s, the Mi'kmaq were encouraged to farm and tend gardens, and many families kept pigs in their backyard all year to be butchered in the fall. The meat was then preserved by salting in wooden barrels, and stored for longer periods. The preserved pork offered an important source of protein during the winter months.

As its name implies, salt pork can be quite salty, so it is usually boiled to extract most of the salt before cooking with it. After boiling, the meat can be grilled or fried and then added to a one-pot meal as with qonesuwey. If salt pork is not readily at hand, it can easily be prepared by coating two parts fresh pork belly strips with a mixture of one part kosher salt, plus a handful of white sugar. Layer the strips in a glass bowl, sprinkling them generously on each side with the mixture. After two days the meat can be wiped clean with a paper towel and used in any recipe without boiling it first.

While we were picking potatoes in Maine, the boss would give us chickens because he raised some on the farm and Mum always cooked them up for a Sunday roast. So many people would come over for dinner—because they knew she was a fantastic cook—that my dad would joke with her, "Wow, I didn't know you had such a large family!"–Anita Francis

When using beef or fresh pork, it is key to make sure the meat is nicely browned in a frying pan or pot with butter or oil, to enrich the dish with that caramelized flavour. The pan can then be deglazed, building flavour when the remaining fried bits and juices are incorporated into the broth in which the potatoes are boiled.

Anita learned this recipe from her mother, Mary Katherine, when they went potato harvesting in Bridgewater, Maine, in late summer and early fall. It is ideal for a main course, and Four Cents offers a useful vehicle for sopping up its rich sauce.

1 tbsp (15 ml) oil,
   butter, or margarine
1.1 lb (500 g) pork
   chops, beef strip
   steaks, or salt pork
   soaked overnight
2 cups (500 ml) water
1 onion, sliced
4 potatoes, sliced
salt and pepper,
   to taste

Qonesuwey (Stew) RECIPE

Heat oil in a deep-frying pan on high heat. When it is hot and shimmering, add meat, reduce the heat to medium, and fry until thoroughly brown on both sides.

Add water to the pan. Using a wooden spoon, scrape the bottom to ensure that all brown bits come up to be mixed in with the broth. Add onion and potatoes, and season with salt and pepper. Cover the pan and return the heat to maximum until the mixture boils, and then reduce to medium for 20 minutes, keeping it covered.

To serve, ladle a chop or steak into a bowl, add a few pieces of potato, and cover with half a ladle or so of broth. Accompany with fresh bread, Lu'sknikn (see p. 99), or (especially) Four Cents (see p. 100).

Pronounced "On-e-se-way," meaning coming from or belonging to the Qonesk, those who make leggings from moose legs from Eskikewa'kik (skin dressers' territory), this dish vaguely resembles a meal cooked elsewhere in the Maritimes called boiled dinner, or *bouilli* among the Acadian population. But Anita Francis and her community's approach to it is quite different in that the dish simmers in much less broth, allowing the flavours to concentrate and meld together beautifully.

Pipnaqn
(Homemade White Bread)
Gertrude Nicholas

Gertrude's upbringing in Indian Island underlines the intercultural challenges facing people from her community. At home, she spoke Mi'kmaq with her family, but as she neared school age, her parents began to speak with the children in English so that they would have an easier time adjusting. But when she and her older brother Garfield arrived for the first day of school in Richibucto, the language of instruction was French—nobody knew any English! This was a reality in the mid-twentieth century when a small percentage of Francophones could speak English, and an even smaller percentage of Anglophones knew French.

Gertrude and her siblings boarded in town during the week, and a taxi brought them back to Indian Island for the weekends. With such a large family at home, her mother, Laura Barlow, made bread often and in large batches using an entire sack of flour (about ten kilos). She never measured, so for sixteen loaves she would start with a few litres of water, two handfuls of sugar, a handful of salt, and a yeast cake. Once the yeast was active and bubbling, her mother blended in leftover bacon grease, near room temperature but still in liquid form, along with any little remaining bacon pieces. Adding fat to the bread helps give it a moist texture. If there was no grease that day, she would substitute lard. Then, she added as much flour as was needed to form a large ball of dough that could be turned out onto a floured surface and kneaded.

Times were so hard that my father had to join the army because my grandmother couldn't feed the whole family when he was just becoming an adult. But he was too skinny and wasn't allowed to enlist, although they gave him a certain amount of time to gain some weight. The problem was he didn't have the means to obtain extra food. One day a friend of his told him, "I know how you can gain weight really fast—buy a whole bunch of bananas, eat them, and then go for your weigh-in." It seemed to do the trick because, sure enough, they took him.
–Gertrude Nicholas

Laura's approach to kneading such a large quantity was to use the entire dining room table. She would create a pillar of dough that extended from one end to the other, and then she, along with Gertrude and her siblings, would together knead the dough for about an hour until it was ready for its first rise. The bread was then baked throughout the day, with half the pans in the oven and the remainder awaiting their second rise.

When Gertrude makes this recipe today, she prepares it with the method and quantities that her mother used. She then shares the loaves with her family and friends. Many people from Indian Island and Elsipogtog remember their mothers and grandmothers making a dozen or more loaves at a time and then storing them in a large barrel for consumption and sharing throughout the week.

We have prepared a smaller recipe, having approximated Laura's measurements.

Pipnaqn RECIPE

Yields 2 loaves
Preparation time:
4 hours, 15 minutes

- -

2 packages active dry yeast
3 tbsp (45 ml) sugar, divided
1/4 cup (60 ml) oil
3 tbsp (45 ml) lard, shortening, or butter
2 tbsp (30 ml) salt
10–11 cups (1.25–2.5L) all-purpose flour
3 1/2 cups (875 ml) lukewarm water
1 tbsp (15 ml) oil
dab butter, optional

Fill a large bowl with lukewarm water, add yeast and 1 tsp (5 ml) sugar and let rest for 15–20 minutes until yeast is active and bubbling.

Meanwhile, in a small microwaveable bowl, mix oil and lard and warm for 30 seconds until lard melts. Add remaining sugar and salt to fat mixture and blend well. If oil is still hot, let it cool until warm so the heat doesn't harm yeast mixture.

Pour mixtures together and mix well with a large wooden spoon until all ingredients are incorporated evenly.

Slowly add flour, a cup at a time, and water, as needed, using the wooden spoon to blend it in. Continue mixing until the dough comes together to form a shaggy ball and no longer sticks to the edges or to the wooden spoon. The more vigorously you stir in flour, the smoother and more elastic the dough will be.

It is fine not to use all the flour, as humidity and moisture levels vary depending on one's kitchen or geographical location, and we advise against pouring in all of it at once, as over-flouring the dough will make it difficult to work with at the next stage.

Let dough rest for 20–30 minutes; this will help to ensure that the water gets absorbed by the flour.

Turn dough onto a floured surface. Have a cup or so flour ready to use if dough becomes sticky. Knead for at least 10 minutes. The dough should become smooth and no longer stick to your hands or surfaces. Toward the end of kneading, no more flour should be necessary.

Grease a large bowl with 1 tbsp (15 ml) oil and leave dough there to rise. Cover the bowl with a dishcloth and put in a warm place, such as in a cold oven with the light turned on. Let rise for an hour or until double in size. Then, punch dough down and cover again with a dishcloth for its second rise (about 45 minutes).

Preheat the oven to 350°F (175°C). Be sure there is no dough still rising in the oven!

Gently turn dough out onto a floured surface and divide into two.

Grease two bread pans with lard or butter. Gently shape dough into a loaf using your hands, and place in the pans. Cover pans with a damp cloth and let dough rise again for 45 minutes on top of the stove until roughly doubled in size.

Bake for about 45 minutes until it browns on top.

Remove bread from the oven, turn loaves out onto a rack to cool, and, if desired, dab butter on the surface while it is still hot—this will make it shiny and also ensure that the crust is soft. Let the bread completely cool before slicing.

Gertrude shares that when her mother had extra bread dough, she made **cinnamon rolls** by rolling out the leftover dough on a table greased with bacon fat. Then, she would spread margarine or butter on the dough, sprinkle a layer of brown sugar, a generous amount of cinnamon, and crushed hazelnuts or walnuts on top. Laura then rolled the dough gently so that it formed a log. She cut the roll into several 1-inch- (2.5-cm-) wide slices, pinwheel style, and arranged them in a well-greased pan. After letting them rise for 45 minutes, covered with a dishcloth, Laura baked these rolls for 15 minutes at 350°F (175°C) until golden.

Homemade Beans

Marlene Thomas

Many Atlantic Canadians use molasses and brown sugar, and often bacon, for their homemade beans. The sugar helps other ingredients darken and caramelize as the beans cook for several hours. In Elsipogtog, however, community-wide health considerations have reshaped how this dish is prepared. By omitting the sugary ingredients, or at least reducing the amount, it is a suitable recipe for anybody with diabetes.

As a result, the colour of the beans is lighter, which is why they are called Ghosty Beans in Indian Island, especially when they are made with white navy beans. Beans are traditionally cooked on Saturdays, starting first thing in the morning so they're ready for suppertime, accompanied by freshly baked Pipnaqn (or tea biscuits and Four Cents), fish cakes, pork chops, sausage, or even hot dogs.

We used to have caribou on Prince Edward Island. But while we were growing up, they had all been hunted, so we didn't eat them anymore.
–Marlene Thomas

Like many of her peers, Marlene Thomas was taken as a child to **Shubenacadie Indian Residential School**—often referred to as "Shubie" by community members. Her husband, Joseph Thomas, managed to avoid Shubie when his grandmother fended the authorities off with a butcher knife.

Whether you decide to include the molasses or not, make sure you have added all the raw ingredients and seasonings you desire before you start cooking. Adding onions toward the end, for example, won't allow them to incorporate into the dish adequately from both a flavour and textural perspective. They need to simmer for a long time on low heat. Marlene makes her beans on the stovetop, but others choose to use a Dutch oven or slow cooker, which will triple the cooking time for this recipe.

Homemade Beans RECIPE

Serves 4–6
Preparation time:
4 hours (+ time to
soak the beans)

- -

1 lb (450 g) dry navy
   or yellow-eye beans
1/2 lb (225 g) salt pork,
   cubed
1/2 tsp (2 ml) pepper
1 tbsp (15 ml) vinegar
1 onion, sliced
   (optional)
1 tsp (5 ml) dry
   mustard
1 cup (250 ml)
   molasses (optional)
3/4 cup (175 ml)
   ketchup (optional)

Soak beans in cold water overnight, then drain.

Place all ingredients in a large pot and add cold water to cover.

Cover pot, place on stove on high heat until it comes to a boil. Then reduce the heat to low and let simmer for 3 hours. Alternatively, use a Dutch oven or slow cooker to bake the beans at 350°F (175°C) for 9 hours.

Goes well with Pipnaqn (p. 109), Tea Biscuits (p. 104), Four Cents (p. 100), or Fish Cakes (p. 10).

Marlene is a master quill artist, which means she works with porcupine quills that she dyes with bright colours and manipulates them by weaving them together into shapes to create lovely objects—from earrings to regalia. She lives in Prince Edward Island, but there are no porcupines on the island—nor bears or moose—unlike on the mainland. She and her supporters collect porcupines from New Brunswick whenever the opportunity presents itself. But it would be dangerous to collect live porcupines, so the trick is to look for them at the side of the road after sunrise when they have been most active and, consequently, get hit by trucks. Marlene collects their freshly killed bodies, brings them home, and cleans them, carefully removing each quill. They are then soaked and stewed in an array of vibrantly coloured liquids to produce beautiful quills that can then be worked into her much-coveted pieces.

Mi'giju' Susie Ann's Chocolate Chip Cookies

Lee Ann Sock

The history of chocolate in Sikniktuk shows the influence of colonial elites and trade on the Indigenous diet. It is a good example of
the impact of biocolonialism—the ways that colonialism occurs through
changes to the ecosystem or through the introduction of new species.
While its origins are Indigenous from South America, chocolate was first
encountered by Europeans in the sixteenth century when they invaded
Mexico. By the middle of the century, it had migrated to Europe where it
began to influence the sweeter side of their diets as a hot beverage. Perhaps
not surprisingly, chocolate makes its first appearance in Atlantic Canada

when it was brought by wealthy French (not Acadian) settlers, and later by affluent British settlers in the eighteenth century; it was a luxury and not a staple of the Acadian and Indigenous diet.

It wasn't until the nineteenth century that chocolate became something to eat, rather than drink, and a standard baking ingredient that was more affordable to broader sectors of society. Some of the country's most well-known candy brands and producers of chocolate, such as Ganong, come from this region and date from the 1800s. Cocoa powder made its way into the ingredients procured at many residential schools, although chocolate bars and cooking chocolate remained a luxury and not part of monthly rations provided by the Indian Agent.

The generosity of community members when they shared dishes that contained luxury items such as chocolate characterizes Mi'giju' Susie Ann's spirit. Her influence on Elsipogtog's festive culinary traditions cannot be understated. She was such a great cook that people would give her their recipes and she would shape them into popular community favourites. Gertrude Nicholas points to Lillian Joseph's cherry marshmallow square recipe, which she entrusted to Mi'giju' Susie Ann. She took it to the next level by using both red and green candied cherries as well as nuts and coconut. She added texture with graham wafers, all of which she further sweetened with condensed milk. This dish is now a Christmas staple in the community.

My mother, Susie Ann, learned to cook from her mother, so she could make all the traditional dishes we grew up with, but she also learned to cook while still in school and worked alongside another lady there. That might be one reason why she became such a generous cook—she was already feeding half the neighbourhood!
–Lee Ann Sock

When Mi'giju' Susie Ann got older, she wasn't able to cook as much as she once did. This compelled the family to sit down with her to record their favourite recipes, including this one for her chocolate chip cookies. Mi'giju' Susie Ann can be considered something of an archive of Elsipogtog's culinary history and her recipes remain cherished in the community.

Mi'giju' Susie Ann's Chocolate Chip Cookies

RECIPE

Preheat oven to 350°F (175°C).

Cream together butter or margarine with brown sugar, then incorporate eggs until evenly blended.

In a separate bowl, combine baking soda, salt, and flour.

Combine dry ingredients into wet ingredients. Add milk and beat until well mixed. Then fold in chocolate chips.

Drop spoon-sized balls onto a greased cookie sheet and bake for 10–15 minutes. When golden, remove to a rack to cool before enjoying.

Yields about 24 cookies
Preparation time: 45 minutes

- -

1/2 cup (125 ml) butter or margarine (room temperature)
1 1/2 cup (375 ml) brown sugar
2 eggs
1 1/2 tsp (7 ml) baking soda
1/2 tsp (2 ml) salt
2 cups (500 ml) all-purpose flour
1/2 cup (125 ml) milk
1 cup (250 ml) chocolate chips

Edward Peterpaul recalls how central cookies seemed to be to his trips to Moncton with his grandmother to sell baskets or wreaths. While there, they would procure things to either make their trip more comfortable, or to bring home to Elsipogtog. They would board a train near Elsipogtog bound for Moncton and head across from the Moncton train station to Highfield Square.

Businesses in Moncton could be very generous to them. Marven's Biscuit Works (established in 1905), for example, would give him a big box of cookies, along with a bunch of bread—stock that they couldn't sell and would otherwise go to waste. Residents of Riverview, who took Edward and his grandmother in for the night, would give him milk and cookies—and his grandmother tea and bread. Edward loved going to Moncton because he always associated it with sweet treats!

Mi'giju' Susie Ann's Peanut Butter Cookies

Lee Ann Sock

Like chocolate, peanuts originate from Indigenous cultures elsewhere in the world. The Incas in Peru, for example, would grind peanuts to make a paste and offer to the dead to sustain them in the afterlife. In Brazil, Indigenous groups mixed that paste or oil with maize to make a beverage, so when Europeans encountered this nutritious, if simple, nut, they found it being used in complex ways. Peanuts were subsequently introduced into the Atlantic Canadian diet by Europeans after they had become part of the European diet, and today they are cultivated in some parts of North America.

You always knew it was harvest season when the house filled with the scent of vinegar. My mother would pickle or jar everything—beets, chow chow, salmon—anything that could be preserved. So, we always had ingredients at their tastiest even in the dead of winter. –Lee Ann Sock

Peanut butter was first patented in Canada by Marcellus Gilmore Edson of Montreal in 1884. Cereal maker Kellogg began selling peanut butter shortly thereafter. Peanut butter's pathway to becoming a staple is complicated. Kellogg first developed peanut butter in order to feed sanatorium patients because once ground it's quite easy to digest and its fat and protein content make it a cheap substitute for meat. With meat rationing during the First and Second World Wars, many families turned to peanut butter for adequate nutrition.

Peanuts and peanut butter were never given to families by the Indian Agent. Like chocolate and vanilla, these items were considered luxuries that only became a common kitchen staple in the last few decades.

The incorporation of peanut butter into Indigenous diets as a protein substitute has a darker side. With the right and ability to fish and hunt being curtailed by settler governments—a direct result of colonization—peanut butter for the most part has become a processed food that, like other processed foods, helps to perpetuate a less healthy lifestyle in comparison with the traditional foodways of the Mi'kmaq. Many peanut butters on the market today—especially the low- to mid-priced ones—contain sugars, salts, and stabilizers that are absent from more expensive varieties that contain just the star ingredient—peanuts. In the balance, Mi'kmaw traditional sources of foods include lean, low-fat varieties of protein, making peanut butter a less-than–ideal replacement for meat.

Mi'giju' Susie Ann's Peanut Butter Cookies

RECIPE

Preheat oven to 350°F (175°C).

Beat together vanilla, peanut butter, shortening, sugar, and eggs until they are well blended.

In a separate bowl, combine flour, baking soda, and salt. Then, gradually mix dry ingredients into wet ingredients until the dough becomes a ball.

Using a spoon, scoop small balls of cookie dough, place on a greased cookie sheet, and flatten with a fork.

Bake for 12–15 minutes, then remove to a rack to cool before sharing and enjoying.

Yields about
24 cookies
Preparation time:
45 minutes

- - - - - - - - - - - - - - - - - - - -

1 tsp (5 ml) vanilla
1 cup (250 ml) peanut
  butter
1 cup (250 ml)
  shortening
2 cups (500 ml)
  brown sugar, lightly
  packed
2 eggs
3 cups (750 ml) flour
1 tsp (5 ml) baking
  soda
1/4 tsp (1 ml) salt

Malia'nji'jewey
(Corn and Potato Casserole)

Doris Copage

Doris Copage's parents raised her and her four sisters and five brothers. Her mother's philosophy for cooking was to make use of whatever you have on hand. She picked vegetables in late summer and always had jars of chow chow, pickles, relish, and tomatoes that pair well with Lu'sknikn (see p. 99) and dishes such as this casserole.

As well as Lu'sknikn, her mother always kept a pot of soup on the stove. It did not always have meat in it, but there would be potatoes, carrots, and turnips—vegetables that store well for year-round consumption. To provide depth, she'd incorporate lard or even shortening into the soup.

Anyone who came over, be they conducting repairs on the house or business with Doris's father, was offered a bowl or two along with Four Cents (see p. 100), which she'd fry up right away for the visitor. Doris recalls how one day a visitor from Red Bank, after a couple bowls, asked "Ma'am, can I ask you a question? What do you call this soup, it's so good!" to which her mother replied, "We call it Poor Man's Soup."

Doris's mum was doing what anybody in her community would do when visitors came to the house. Mi'kmaw hospitality is an important aspect of the cultural traditions with which Doris was raised and it remains visible throughout Sikniktuk today.

The ingredients for this recipe manifest the blending of traditional and settler foodways in communities such as Elsipogtog. Both potatoes and corn are Indigenous sources of food in the area. Today corn grown in the region is usually destined to feed cows and pigs.

My mum used to teach cooking to the young women in our community. They rented the hall once a week and she'd teach them recipes such as Indian Bread or Lu'sknikn. There's this one woman down the road who still makes it the way my mum used to. –Doris Copage

Most people don't remember a lot of corn growing in their grandparents' gardens, but when it was planted, the cobs would be harvested, peeled, and hung to dry. Like the canned corn used in this recipe, dried corn could be stored throughout the cooler months for soups and casseroles where the dish's broth would soften the corn, creating a welcomed fresh flavour.

Serves 4
Preparation time:
65 minutes

----

6 potatoes, sliced
2 onions, sliced
2 cans creamed corn
1 tbsp (15 ml) parsley
salt and pepper, to
    taste
1 box Ritz crackers,
    crushed
1 tbsp (15 ml) oil
4 thin pork chops or
    a dozen hot dogs/
    breakfast sausages

Malia'nji'jewey RECIPE

Preheat oven to 350°F (175°C).

Place potatoes and onions in a pot, and cover with water. Bring to a boil on medium heat for 10 minutes. The water level will decrease; do not add more.

Add corn (with its water), parsley, and salt and pepper to the pot. Blend in crackers until they are evenly distributed.

Pour mixture into a deep casserole dish 13- x 8-inch (33- x 20-cm) and bake for 30 minutes.

In the meantime, pour oil into a frying pan, place on high heat, and fry meat for 3 minutes on each side.

Remove casserole from the oven and position meat on top before returning it to the oven and baking for another 15 minutes until golden brown.

This dish can be served with Lu'sknikn (see p. 99) and Chow Chow (see p. 62) or pickled beets.

Strawberry shortcake.

Food and Community Celebrations

Like the potlatch in western Canada, Indigenous celebrations and cultural traditions such as the powwow (mawiomi) were discouraged by the federal government just decades ago. Along with them went singing, dancing, crafts, arts, intergenerational knowledge transmission, and spiritual practices. That was the idea, but the resilience of the Mi'kmaq means that they found other ways to gather to celebrate their culture.

One such example is the annual celebration of Saint Anne, the patron saint of the Mi'kmaq, on July 28. The community gathers at the church of this name in Elsipotog and pray; they also hold a church picnic, to which all are invited—including settlers from neighbouring communities. Everybody contributes food to the gathering—roasted chicken with stuffing, a variety of salads, lobster, and many kinds of fish. Anita Joseph

A tray of Lu'sknikn set up at Lennox Island powwow.

specifically associates strawberry shortcake with this celebration, given the timing of that fruit's harvest.

Long rows of tables are set up so that people can sit down and share a meal. A committee of volunteers runs the event, which they also use to raise money for the church. It is a huge festivity—organizers often spend the night in the church hall so that work can resume first thing in the morning. This celebration typically lasts two to three days and involves a procession that ends at the church where the statue of Saint Anne stands, after which a mass is said in her honour.

The Sunday meal is another, more regular, form of celebration. Everybody went to church first, however, which usually wrapped up in time for the mid-day or afternoon meal that featured a large piece of meat and all the trimmings. Typically, the mother or grandmother would get the roast in the oven before going to church so that it would be ready when they returned.

As Lulu Sock points out, years ago the community hosted picnics that also lasted two to three days and featured dancing, just as a powwow today would. People from all over the region came to the celebration to watch, take part, and to engage with Mi'kmaw culture and history. Some people think these picnics stopped due to a lack of volunteerism as people had to organize the event, invite dancers, decorate, and of course prepare food. But with the resurgence of powwows, there is now a circuit of celebrations that happens throughout Mi'kma'ki—and North America—that attracts people from near and far.

Powwows take place throughout Sikniktuk, especially in Elsipogtog, but also increasingly at Mount Allison University and other settler institutions. While the purpose and focus is on Mi'kmaw culture, foodways are celebrated through the appearance of food trucks selling popular Indigenous (L'nu) tacos, and the quintessential hot dogs and hamburgers that the Mi'kmaq associate with celebrations.

Glossary of Mi'kmaq Terms

Amlamgog: Fort Folly First Nation; also referred to as Kwesawek.

Eel Ground First Nation: Natoaganeg. Natuamk is spearing eels through the ice.

Embubgek: "river that flows out." Bepge'g is the town of Richibucto because it is located downriver from Elsipogtog First Nation. Pi'taw is upriver, and so the village of Bass River and other upriver towns are also called Pi'taw. Embubgek implies movement downriver.

Esgenoopetiitj First Nation: "lookout point," a place where people can wait for paddlers coming in from Epekwitk (Prince Edward Island).

Eskikewa'kik: "skin dressers' territory," like Sikniktuk, one of the seven Mi'kmaq traditional districts; located on Nova Scotia's Eastern Shore.

Gaqpesaq: smelts.

Gaspalaw: salted herring.

Gatow (as in John Gatow)**:** eel.

Lno Minigoo: Indian Island First Nation. Its name translates to Indian (lno) Island (mnigoo).

L'nu Mniku: Lennox Island First Nation.

L'nu taco: Indigenous taco.

Lu'sknikn: dough that makes a crust; the name comes from elu'sknmn, the action of kneading the dough.

Malia'nji'jewey: corn and potato casserole; it means "Little Malian's" in reference to its originator, Mi'giju' Malian.

Mawiomi: powwow or gathering.

Metepenagiag: Red Bank First Nation, although Elder Gary Simon, citing Elder George Paul, relates that Metepena'giag means "High Bank" whereas Megwebena'giag means "Red Bank."

Midisaqamiktuk: a camp site near Elsipogtog First Nation, previously known as Big Cove—so named because miti (poplar trees) grow there.

Mi'giju': grandmother.

Mi'kma'ki: land of the Mi'kmaq.

Mimgwaqn: acorns.

Mitji: let's eat.

Nijinjk: salmon eggs or roe.

Nsukwi: aunt.

Peju: cod.

Pipnaqn: homemade bread.

Plaqawej: grouse or partridge.

Poggwitewe'l: Mi'kmaq appropriation of the English term, buckwheat pancakes.

Qonesk: "those who makes leggings from moose legs;" this word is a nickname for "those from Eski'kewaq." Eski'kewaq is one of the seven regions of Mi'kma'ki. According to legend, two L'nu'k hunters killed a moose and divided it up; one took the bottom cut of the legging hide to make moccasins (qunes) and the other took the top cut of the hide to make leggings (tmetkwesikn).

Salite: auction to help with funeral expenses; the word might be Mi'kmaw slang for "sale day."

Sikniktuk: one of the seven regions of the Mi'kmaq; the name means "drainage land."

Sipekne'katik: Indian Brook First Nation; the name means "land of the ground nut potatoes."

Sisla'gwa'taqn: anything fried, or fry bread.

Sitmug: beach.

Skodagon: a mixture (root vegetables as a side for dinner, for example); the term also means "cow's cud."

Tapitatk: potatoes.

Tjipogtotig: Bouctouche First Nation. Bouctouche is a French adaptation of Puktukji'j, meaning "Little Grand Harbour."

Tupsi: dogwood used to weave chairs, baskets, etc. The bark makes a good tea for treating skin ailments.

Wapus: white rabbit, originating from the wape'k, meaning "white." A brown rabbit is apli'kmuj.

Wenuj tia'm: beef or "French moose," from French (wenuj) and moose (tia'm). Ground beef is nukwa'kittasik wejutia'muwey, whereas ground moose is nukwa'kittasik tia'muwey.

Witjiboti: bag strapped to Mi'giju's hip with supplies.

Wiusey petaqn: meat pie.

Index

Entries in **bold** refer to recipes.
Page numbers in *italics* refer to images.

squirrels 95
strawberries 12, 14, 26–27, 33, 95
  strawberry shortcake *123*, 124
Stuffed Salmon 28, 30
Swiss Steak with Moose Meat *54, 55,* 56–57

T

Tea Biscuits 83, *102, 103, 104,* 113–14
Three Sisters 97. *See also* corn, squash
Tjipogtotig (Bouctouche First Nation) vii
tomatoes 3, 12, 22, 57, 60, 97
  Annie's Soup 84–85
  Barley Soup *81*
  green 62
    Chow Chow 61
treaty rights (Mi'kmaq) viii, 40–41, 57, 86, 118.
       See also Marshall Decision; Marshall,
       Donald Jr.
  Peace and Friendship Treaties 37
trout 11, 96
tuna 10
turkey 59, 78
turnip 63, 76, 87–88, 120
  Boiled Dinner with Neck Bones 74, *76*
  Rabbit Stew 86, *87,* 88

U

Uncle Herman's Partridge Stew 58–59

W

white fish 10, 21–22
  Chowder (Lobster, Clam, or Corn) 10, 21–22
Wiusey Petaqn (Meat Pie with Pork) 78–79

Index of Names